Hard-Nosed Advice
from a Cranky Law Professor

Hard-Nosed Advice
from a Cranky Law Professor

How to Succeed in Law School

Second Edition

Cristina C. Knolton

Professor of Legal Analysis, Writing, and Skills
Southwestern Law School

Lisa C. Dennis

Associate
Fagen, Friedman & Fulfrost LLP

Austen L. Parrish

Dean and James H. Rudy Professor of Law
Indiana University Maurer School of Law

CAROLINA ACADEMIC PRESS

Durham, North Carolina

Library of Congress Cataloging-in-Publication Data

Names: Parrish, Austen L., author. | Knolton, Cristina C., author. |
    Dennis, Lisa C., author.
Title: Hard-nosed advice from a cranky law professor : how to succeed in
    law school / Cristina C. Knolton, Lisa C. Dennis, Austen L. Parrish.
Description: Second edition. | Durham, North Carolina : Carolina Academic
    Press, 2021. | Includes index.
Identifiers: LCCN 2021015187 (print) | LCCN 2021015188 (ebook) | ISBN
    9781531022303 (paperback) | ISBN 9781531022310 (ebook)
Subjects: LCSH: Law--Study and teaching--United States. | Law
    students--United States--Handbooks, manuals, etc.
Classification: LCC KF283 .P37 2021 (print) | LCC KF283 (ebook) | DDC
    340.071 / 173--dc23
LC record available at https://lccn.loc.gov/2021015187
LC ebook record available at https://lccn.loc.gov/2021015188

Carolina Academic Press
700 Kent Street
Durham, North Carolina 27701
Telephone (919) 489-7486
Fax (919) 493-5668
www.cap-press.com
Printed in the United States of America

CONTENTS

———————————

ACKNOWLEDGMENTS

We are grateful to those who read and commented on this book during its many drafts and for the support of Southwestern Law School. Thank you to our Southwestern colleagues for their ideas and encouragement. Thank you to Bridgette de Gyarfas, Courtney Martin, and Natalie Rodriguez for their valuable suggestions. Thank you to our students, including Mouna Kezbar, Elijah Lichtenberg, Eric Geier, Brian Luper, Para Noh, and Jessica Priel for their research assistance and suggestions. And, lastly, special thanks to Ryland Bowman and Kathleen Soriano Taylor for their skilled and thoughtful attention to detail in polishing the final edits to the book.

ABOUT THE AUTHORS

Cristina C. Knolton: Professor Knolton is a Professor of Legal Writing, Analysis and Skills at Southwestern Law School. Prior to joining Southwestern, Professor Knolton taught at Texas Tech University School of Law and LaVerne College of Law. In addition to legal writing and analysis, Professor Knolton has taught the subjects of negotiation, alternative dispute resolution, property, contracts, and marital property.

Professor Knolton is currently the co-director of the Negotiation Honors Program at Southwestern and coaches Southwestern's Negotiation teams. Professor Knolton was the inaugural recipient of the Professor Anahid Gharakhanian Excellence in Teaching Award. She has spoken before academic and professional forums on topics such as "Incorporating Exams into the Legal Writing Classroom," "How to Succeed in Law School," "Texas Community Property Law," "A Lawyer's Role as an Advocate in the Legal System," "The Deal," and "Negotiation Tactics in Criminal Defense."

After completing her law degree at the University of Texas, where she was a member of the Texas Law Review, Professor Knolton began her legal career as a real estate attorney at the firm of Akin, Gump, Strauss, Haeur & Feld in San Antonio, Texas, representing commercial real estate clients in the acquisition, sale, ownership, and leasing of income-producing properties. She has also served as a volunteer mediator for the Lubbock County Alternative Dispute Resource Center.

Lisa C. Dennis: Ms. Dennis is an associate at the firm Fagen Friedman & Fulfrost LLP, where she represents clients in special education and student issues. Ms. Dennis has practiced in the area of special education law for eight years, and has expertise in all aspects of this area, including matters related to the IDEA and Section 504 of the Rehabilitation Act, special education proceedings, IEP meetings, manifestation determination meetings, as well as due process mediations, hearings before the Office of Administrative Hearings and appeals from OAH decisions in U.S. District Court. She also has extensive experience supporting clients in the area of student discipline, in responding to UCP complaints, and Public Records Act requests.

Prior to joining the firm, Ms. Dennis was affiliated with a boutique law firm in the Pasadena area specializing in special education matters. She brings a unique perspective to her legal practice, having begun her professional career as an educator. For nearly 20 years, Ms. Dennis taught social students and English in publish high schools near Los Angeles and in the Bay Area.

Ms. Dennis earned her Juris Doctor from University of La Verne College of Law and Holds a B.A. in history from the University of California, Berkeley, as well as a secondary teaching credential in social studies and English from Mills College.

Austen L. Parrish: Dean Parrish is the Dean and James H. Rudy Professor at Indiana University Bloomington's Maurer School of Law. Previously he served as interim dean and CEO (2012–2014), vice dean (2008–2012), and the Irwin R. Buchalter Professor of Law (2007–2008) at Southwestern Law School in Los Angeles. From 2003 to 2010, he directed Southwestern's international and comparative summer law program in Vancouver, Canada, hosted by the University of British Columbia Faculty of Law in collaboration with the International Centre for Criminal Law Reform and Criminal Justice Policy, a United Nations affiliate

Over his career, he has taught a variety of courses, including Civil Procedure, Constitutional Law, Federal Courts, Transnational Law, International Environmental Law, and Public International Law. He serves on the Board of Directors for AccessLex Institute and a member of the Executive Committee for the Association of American Law Schools. He also serves as a member of the AALS Deans Steering Committee. Prior to entering academia, he was an attorney with O'Melveny & Myers in Los Angeles. Dean Parrish earned his B.A. from the University of Washington, in Seattle, and his J.D. from Columbia Law School, where he was a Harlan Fiske Stone Scholar.

INTRODUCTION

The idea of approaching law school in a traditional manner is out of vogue. No one right way exists, or so we are told, on how to learn. Students have many different perspectives, depending on their cultural and economic background, as well as where, when, and in what order they were born. Students are often advised that the path to success changes depending on whether they are a Baby Boomer, a Tweener, a Gen X'r, or a Millennial. For many then, the way to achieve success in law school is a personal thing. Students are encouraged to do whatever they feel most comfortable with and to embrace what works for them. Each student has their own way of doing well, and every rule can be bent or broken.

This book takes a different approach. It provides no-nonsense, sometimes hard-nosed, advice that is intended to cut across generations. Students learn in different ways. However, regardless of a student's background, law professors expect specific things. A student either figures out what the professor wants, or is left behind. Doing what "is comfortable" or what "works for you" is bad advice, because when students begin law school they have no idea what works, and the first year of law school is not a comfortable experience. In short, if a student wishes to excel, there are right ways to approach law school. This book explains—hopefully in a straightforward way—what some of those ways are.

The information presented here is intended to help students understand what law professors expect of them. In a straight-talking fashion, each chapter instructs students on how to give themselves the best chance of doing well. The book covers those tasks that students commonly face in law school: from reading and briefing cases, to outlining, to preparing and taking exams, to being called on in class. The book also provides advice on success outside the classroom. In many ways, the book promotes professionalism and common sense.

This book distinguishes itself in two ways. First, many law school preparation guides are hundreds of pages long and purport to anticipate every tidbit of information an aspiring law student might wish to know, no matter how tangential. Few students read those books cover to cover, and the advice they provide is often, at best, only marginally useful. In contrast, this is a short book. It is not, and is not intended to be, an exhaustive guide to all things law school related. It attempts to be concise and to the point: an accessible book that can be read quickly and provide useful and practical advice on how to approach law school. Second, the advice that some preparation books provide suggests students succeed only by mastering some closely-guarded secret, which law professors know but conspiratorially refuse to reveal. This book rejects that sort of nonsense. Students succeed in law school not through short cuts and tricks, but through hard work. This book provides concrete advice on the fundamentals that students must master to do well.

Hard-Nosed Advice
from a Cranky Law Professor

PREPARING FOR LAW SCHOOL

Getting Ready for the First Year

Welcome. So you think you want to go to law school? Good. I like seeing new faces. Students keep me feeling young. In the next hour, I will tell you what law school is all about, what you need to do to get ready. Listen carefully. Getting off to a good start is critical.

A. A Little Perspective

You need to be prepared for law school, but perhaps not in the way you suspect. Students are now told that they must do many things before the first day of class: from reading law books and outlining cases to perusing legal philosophy. Absolute nonsense. Your entire undergraduate education is your preparation. A few months of futzing around playing "lawyer" is not going to do anything for you.

The school's Admissions Committee believed you were ready for law school or you would not have been admitted. They were willing to take you as you are. They had confidence in you. You should too.

Relax. Yes, that is what you need to do the summer before you start law school. The first year of law school can be stressful. You will be asked to do a tremendous amount of work. You will be pushed harder mentally than you have before. So chill. Take advantage of the time you have left. Hit the beach. Spend time with family. Kick back.

Do not read casebooks. Do not read legal philosophy. Do not read law books. If you want to read something, read this book. Then read the latest bestsellers! That's good prep. That has a much better chance of helping you. In fact, reading a popular book is a good idea. Much of what you do in law school is read. You will need to read more than you have before and getting into the habit of reading every day is good practice.

One more small point: do your best to refrain from emailing your professors in the summer to introduce yourself and explain how excited you are to be in their class. Your professors know you are excited for law school. Don't be the eager beaver. You will fare better by showing your excitement through your preparation for class.

B. Use the Summer Before Wisely

There are a few things that are essential to do before law school. First, despite my earlier advice, if your school offers a legal writing course or an introduction to law school course over the summer, take it. Many incoming students find these courses helpful. Schools often design these courses to give students a leg up before they arrive. Some schools will offer a summer academic support program to teach incoming students how to brief cases, create outlines, and participate in class. If you have the opportunity to participate in these type of courses seize the opportunity. They will make your transition from college to law school easier.

Second, and more importantly, get your personal life in order. If you are moving to a new city, be sure to arrive ahead of time to get settled. Have you figured out your housing? Is it relatively near the school? Is it in a safe area? You will be busy. You do not want to be commuting long distances, if you can help it. If you can live on campus, live there.

C. Prepare Your Family and Friends

You want to prepare your family and friends for the upcoming year. The first year of law school requires sacrifices. Life exists outside of law school, but you also need to ensure your loved ones realize that you are going to be busy.

How do you prepare your family? Have them visit the law school. If there's an orientation, invite them to join you. If you can, have them to sit in on a class. Make them read one of the cases. If they did not go to law school, give them a glimpse of what law school is like — a taste of what you have to go through each day. By the time you are finished, they'll be sending you home-baked cookies and family-care packs and doing your laundry on a weekly basis.

D. Visit the School

You want to hit the ground running, so you might as well visit the school too. Get the lay of the land. Figure out where your classes are. If you think far enough ahead, you can even sit in on a class. Find out where the library is and where the key administrative offices are. Talk to the school's admissions office and ask them for a tour of the school. They are sure to give you one, and it may make the first few days of school easier.

E. Work Out Your Finances

You want to be able to focus on one thing your first year of law school: the first year of law school. You cannot afford to be distracted by worrying about your finances. So — unless you are one of the very few who are independently wealthy and can just write a check to pay for your education — before law school begins set up a meeting with the school's financial aid office. You will want to apply for financial aid, scholarships, grants, and to anyone that is willing to give you money.

Approach law school frugally. You are a student, so live like a student. Create a budget and live as leanly as possible. Get a roommate. Buy used books. Get a lower-rent apartment. Eat in more, eat out less. Keep that old junker of a car, you don't need a new one. You'll thank yourself later.

Credit cards are not a wise method for paying for law school tuition. Credit card interest rates are high, and you will almost always need to start paying them off while you're still in school. Due to the way credit card payments work, you also are at a higher risk of ruining your credit. Speak with your Financial Aid Office at your school, they can explain your options. Using credit cards is not one of them.

The Right Mindset

To do well in law school, you need to understand what getting a juris doctor (J.D.) is all about. Here are the basics.

A. Understand the Point of Law School

When you begin law school, it's helpful to understand what law school is all about and, more importantly, what law school is not about. Law school is not intended to teach solely to the bar exam. The bar exam has little to do with long-term career success. To learn what they test on the bar exam, you will take a bar exam preparation course.

In many ways, law school also is not primarily designed—at least not the first-year courses—to teach you how to become a practicing attorney. Not directly. Most first-year courses are structured to teach you how to do legal analysis, how to read and understand cases and statutes, and how to think creatively, in a sophisticated way, about legal issues. That's it, and, believe me, that is more than enough. In the upper-division, you will have more opportunities to take courses that teach you practical lawyering skills and the ins-and-outs of legal practice. The best schools—and when I say best, I don't mean highest-ranked—will provide you instruction in the upper-division on how to do those tasks that young attorneys most commonly face, from document drafting, to negotiation, to oral advocacy, to client interviewing and counseling.

Law school is also not primarily intended to teach you the law. In class, you will discuss the law, but the primary purpose of discussing the law is the discussion itself: the give and take, the pros and cons, the creative thinking, and the ability to think around and beyond the facts of the case at hand. The process of thinking through and arguing the issues is what class is for. In class you will explore the historical development of the law, the policies that underlie it, and how law reflects fundamental assumptions about ourselves, our society, and our culture. And ultimately, what most professors test for in exams is not some "right" answer, but your ability to do the very kind of analysis involved in class discussions. Law school tests your ability to think through issues presented by the cases and statutes, and to exercise your own judgment about them.

Nor is law school mostly about memorizing black letter law. You'll be tempted to think it is. You'll be wrong. Black letter law consists of those principles in a particular area or field of law (for example, contracts or torts) that are beyond dispute. Black letter law is rarely useful in practice. Lawyers do not fight over legal principles that are free from doubt. Lawyers fight over cases when the law is uncertain. If you want to learn black letter law, become a legal secretary. Anyone can pick up a simple statute and read it, but no client pays for a lawyer who spits back only what they could have looked up for themselves. Being a lawyer requires more. If you want to learn how to challenge the law, how to figure out answers to questions when no law exists, how to develop creative solutions for clients — then you are in the right place.

B. Question Everything

Question everything. Getting in the right mindset means that you will question everything that you read and hear in law school. If you're not questioning, you are not thinking. If you are not thinking, you are not learning. If you are not learning, you might as well go home.

When I say "question everything," I do not mean you should constantly raise your hand. Sure participate, but do it selectively. No one likes a show-off. Your classmates will have a name for those students whose arms seem to get stuck in the air. They call them "gunners." Don't be a gunner, but do question. Don't accept everything your professor says or read your casebooks like a mindless automaton. Think about what is being said. Do you agree? Why? Why not? Is the legal principle you are studying a good one? Who does it benefit? Who doesn't it benefit? What are the law's implications? Why is it the law? Should it be? How does the case demonstrate law in practice? Professors like students who question what they hear and read. Those students will make good lawyers.

C. Accept Ambiguity

In law school, you must accept ambiguity. Often there is no right answer. Don't misunderstand me, there are wrong answers; lots of them. Students consistently give wrong answers when they have not read the material carefully or have failed to understand what they have read. However, many right answers exist. Get used to professors not telling you the answer. They are not being mean. They are not hiding the ball. One right answer rarely exists. It's the nature of law. The best students and the best lawyers understand this. Cases are what you make of them, and so too is the law. You use it for the ends you need it for.

D. Understand the Socratic Method

Ah, the Socratic Method: the bane of every law student's existence. The one thing that sends shivers through and strikes fear in even the most accomplished of students.

What is the Socratic Method? In its classic form, a professor repeatedly asks questions of students to encourage them to more fully understand the topic at hand. The professor will ask questions until a contradiction is exposed in the student's reasoning, thereby proving a fallacy in the student's initial assumptions. To learn an area of law through Socratic discourse, the area is broken down into a series of questions, the answers to which gradually distill information about that area of law. Or, more simply: the Socratic Method means lots of questioning and not much lecturing.

Most law professors no longer use the Socratic Method, at least not as classically understood, and not in its most severe form. The contemporary approach is more of a conversation. Law professors these days use class discussions and light questioning as a way to engage students in a large class and explore difficult and complicated legal issues. Asking students questions and probing their understanding of the material is intended to help develop students' critical thinking skills. Questioning students forces students to analyze legal issues, to reason, and then to think critically about not only their own arguments, but also those made by others. It requires students to be well-prepared and to have read carefully before class. The professor is also forcing the student to articulate, develop, and defend a position that may at first be just an intuition. Professors also try to connect legal reasoning to professional and moral values.

So how does it work? Generally, the professor invites a student to summarize a case assigned for that day's class. Professors will also often ask students, as a way to get the discussion started, to summarize either the facts, issues, holding, or reasoning of the court's decision. Professors expect a cogent and succinct summary. Regardless of the thoroughness of the student's initial response, the professor then pushes the student on details perhaps overlooked or on issues unresolved. A professor will often manipulate the case's facts into a series of hypotheticals and then ask a student whether the court should have ruled differently if the case's facts changed slightly.

Once you understand the purpose of law school, the Socratic Method (or modern variations on it) makes sense. One of law school's primary goals is to equip students with the analytical skills they need to solve legal problems. The law changes and the legal issues students will confront after they graduate can vary tremendously. Teaching students particular pieces of law is of limited value. What professors can do well is help students develop those legal reasoning skills that will aid students when they become lawyers, regardless of the area of practice.

For these reasons, it is critical that you engage fully in the Socratic questioning. You will learn to think like a lawyer by listening not only to the professor's questions, but by listening to your classmates' responses. You need to hear your classmates' response and closely analyze your professor's reaction to those response. What are the professor's facial expressions in response to the student's answer? What follow-up questions is the professor asking? How is your professor deepening your classmates' analysis? Sadly, many students are so worried about the dreaded sound of their name being called out that they stop focusing on what their classmates are saying and instead use that time to prepare themselves for the next topic. Those students are losing the opportunity to learn how their professor wants them to think about the issues. Those students are losing the opportunity to learn how their professor wants them to think about the issues on the exam. If you plan to ace the course, pay attention to each student's answer and the professor's response.

E. Cautiously Use Hornbooks and Commercial Outlines

Hornbooks and treatises contain comprehensive and in-depth discussions of particular areas of the law. Commercial outlines, in contrast, are guides that cover the specific cases and legal rules typically covered in your courses. Commercial outlines present the material in a condensed fashion, and are often designed to mirror the material included in the casebook.

You should use hornbooks, treatises, and commercial outlines, but sparingly. Some people will tell you to buy them right away. Wait. Struggle with the material. Force yourself to read the difficult cases. If you don't, you are short-changing yourself. You are training your brain to take shortcuts.

This does not mean that hornbooks, treatises, and commercial outlines don't have their uses. They are great for filling in the gaps, or if you're confused after class and you need to figure out the answer. If that means going to the library and finding a book that explains what you're covering in class, so be it, but do not expect yourself to read commercial outlines regularly in addition to your regularly assigned material.

F. Create a Schedule

The most important piece of preparation advice I can give you is to get organized. You want to plan out how you're going to spend your days and weeks. You should include in your schedule time for reading, briefing cases, reviewing class notes, preparing for class, outlining, meeting with professors, and taking practice exams. When the semester starts, you should be spending most of your time reading, briefing, and getting ready for class. As the semester ends, you should spend most of your time finishing your outlines and taking practice exams.

During law school, with class time and studying combined, you should be working a full 8–9 hours each day during the week. With lunch and other breaks, that means you're likely putting in a 9–11-hour day. If you can't handle that, then the legal profession may not be right for you. Although not all jobs are this way, many young lawyers regularly work 10–12-hour days, and some many more. The reality is the practice of law is challenging and the economic pressures and deadlines can commonly lead to lost weekends and evenings.

G. Avoid Common Missteps

To succeed in law school also be sure to avoid common missteps. First, the most common mistake made by new students is to view the process as a competition with classmates. Compete only with yourself. Your classmates are your allies and they will certainly be your future colleagues. The legal community is small, and you begin building your reputation when law school begins.

Second, you want to manage stress. This means you should strive for balance. Law school requires a lot of work, but it doesn't mean you should try to study twenty-four hours a day, seven days a week. There will be many ups and downs for you in the first year, and some of you will hit times of self-doubt. But there's more to life that just law school. You can't go through life as a machine. If you like exercising, continue exercising. Be sure to eat right. Get enough sleep and don't completely tune out your friends and family. In fact, make new friends. Loved ones are a natural support system for law school stress. While most friends and family, unless they are lawyers themselves, will not understand how difficult law school can be, they can provide support.

Understanding the First-Year Curriculum

The first-year courses are all foundational. For most schools and most J.D. programs, you will have no choice in your schedule. You must take the courses they tell you. No matter what school you're attending, the first-year courses are likely to be the same: torts, criminal law, contracts, civil procedure, property, and legal writing. So what are they? Here's a very brief overview.

A. Contracts

Assume your uncle promised to pay you $10,000 on your 18th birthday, but when your birthday came, he changed his mind and gave you $100 instead. Can you enforce his original promise and make him pay $10,000? What if he promised to pay you $10,000 if you received straight A's in college? Can this promise be enforced? What is the difference between the two promises? Does it matter if the promises were made in writing? Your contracts course will address these issues, as well as a range of other issues stemming from promises made between parties. Your contracts course will discuss how contracts are formed, what makes particular promises legally binding, justifications for backing out of a contract, and remedies for breach of contractual obligations.

B. Property

Property law is about the relationships among people with respect to things. The course focuses on the ownership of property and rights that accompany that ownership. You will learn about landlord-tenant relationships, easements, conveyance of land, adverse possession ("squatting"), and, of course, every law student's favorite topic: "future interests." You will learn to answer this fascinating questions: will the interest vest, if at all, within 21 years of a life in being? Sound like a bunch of mush? Don't worry. You will become all too familiar with what that means in just a short time. If you ever want to leave the family farm to your grandchildren and their descendants, knowledge of that rule might even come in handy. What if your grandchildren move into the farm and discover a treasure that was buried on the property hundreds of years ago? Do they own it merely because it was found on their property? You will have to wait to find out in your property law course.

C. Criminal Law

Ever hear the words burglary, theft, and robbery and wonder what is the difference? If so, you will likely enjoy this class. Many law students enjoy criminal law. Criminal law deals with crimes and the punishment that accompanies those crimes. What if someone approached you on the street with a knife and told you to hand over your wallet? Do you have the right to react with deadly force? What exactly counts as self-defense? What if you accidently kill someone in a car accident? Is that a crime? Can you go to jail? Your criminal law course will teach you the elements required for crimes and the defenses to those crimes. Most criminal law courses cover homicide crimes, such as murder and manslaughter, theft crimes such as robbery and embezzlement, as well as inchoate crimes such as solicitation and conspiracy. You might also discuss the broader principles of crime, why we punish people, and the effects punishment has on society.

D. Torts

What is a "tort"? That is a question most first-year law students have before stepping into their torts course. A tort is a wrong. Torts is thus the study of wrongful acts. How is this different from criminal law, you ask? Isn't murder also a wrong? Is murder also covered in torts? Not exactly. Murder is certainly wrong, but it is not a tort. It is a crime, punishable by jail. The corresponding wrong in torts is called "wrongful death." Torts are wrongs between two private parties. Torts are punishable by monetary damages, rather than jail time. Thus, if you kill someone, you could go to jail for murder. You can also be sued by the victim's family for monetary damages under the tort "wrongful death." Assault is another tort you may have heard of. There is criminal assault and civil assault. You can go to jail for criminal assault. You can be sued for monetary damages if you commit a civil assault. Criminal assault and civil assault have different requirements (i.e. elements), but if all requirements are met, a person can be both guilty of criminal assault and liable for civil assault (the tort).

Typical torts include anything from rear-ending someone on the highway to punching someone in the face during a bar fight. Torts typically fit into three categories: (i) intentional torts (such as battery, assault, false imprisonment, intentional infliction of emotional distress); (ii) strict liability offenses; and (iii) negligence. You will spend most of your torts course covering negligence. If you are involved in a car accident and the driver who hit you was texting while driving, you are likely to file a negligence claim against the driver because the driver did not act as a reasonable person would under the same circumstances.

E. Civil Procedure

Civil procedure. The name alone might make this course seem technical and unexciting, but it can be fun and it is definitely a critical class to becoming a lawyer. The word "procedure" refers to the procedure, or rules, governing how to actually file a lawsuit and where to file the lawsuit. You can have a winning case for your client, but if you don't know where or how to file the client's case, you will never win. The word "civil" refers to the fact that the rules you will be learning about are the rules for lawsuits between private citizens, rather than criminal lawsuits which involve the government and an individual accused of a crime. The first-year civil procedure course focuses primarily on the rules to file a federal lawsuit; however, many professors reference similarities to state courts as well. Don't worry, you will get to learn about the rules of criminal procedure as well — you just have to wait until your second year of law school.

Let's take an example of what you might learn in civil procedure. Assume a citizen of California is involved in a car accident with a citizen of New Mexico. The car accident takes place in Texas while both parties are on vacation. The California citizen is injured and wants to file a lawsuit against the New Mexico driver. Where should she bring the lawsuit? In California, where she lives? In New Mexico, where the other driver lives? In Texas, where the accident occurred? Does she have to bring the case in State Court or can she bring the case in Federal Court? Your civil procedure class will answer these questions. The course will teach you the rules that govern the civil litigation process, such as jurisdiction, the filing of the initial complaint, types of discovery requests, when to join two cases together, and various types of motions the parties can make to have a case thrown out.

F. Legal Research and Writing

Legal research and writing is arguably the most critical course in the first-year curriculum. Think you already know how to write? Think again. Writing like a lawyer is not like any type of writing you have done before.

Some might even say it is not writing at all. This is a good thing for those who are scared of writing. If you have previously experienced trauma in your writing classes, this is your chance for a fresh start. Often students who have struggled in writing courses in the past are able to succeed in their Legal Writing course.

In essence, your legal research and writing course will teach you how to be a lawyer. Lawyers have to research. They also need to be able to analyze and understand the law they find even when that law was not covered in one of their law school courses. Actually, most legal issues that arise in practice are so specific that the topic was never covered in any of the courses described above. After finding the law and understanding it, lawyers need to be able to write the law down and make persuasive arguments under the law so a court will rule in their favor. Your legal research and writing class teaches you how to do that. There is a specific formula lawyers must use in presenting their arguments. Legal research and writing teaches you how to write in that formula. Your legal research and writing course is so critical to your success, this book devotes an entire chapter just to that subject. So I will stop here. I don't want to spoil the surprise.

Well that's all for now. If you've paid attention, you'll do fine. See you in class. I look forward to it.

Checklist Reminders

To Do the Summer Before:

- ❏ Visit law school, sit in on class
- ❏ Take summer introduction courses (if available)
- ❏ Work out housing (not too costly, close to school)
- ❏ Get personal life in order
- ❏ Prepare family and friends for busy year
- ❏ Meet with financial aid office and arrange finances (apply for scholarships, if not too late)

To Remember in Law School

- ❏ Be inquisitive
- ❏ Be prepared every day

- ❑ *Accept ambiguity*
- ❑ *Use hornbooks, treatises, and commercial outlines very sparingly (don't buy right away)*
- ❑ *Create a schedule for the fall semester (study time, class prep, classes etc.)*
- ❑ *Be supportive of classmates, not competitive (future colleagues)*
- ❑ *Strive for balance (i.e., eat, exercise) — but will be working very hard!*

2

PROFESSOR EXPECTATIONS

Law is a profession; you must act like a professional. If you do not, you will not be in my class for long. Every professor has the same rules, the same basic expectations. They may not admit it, but they do. Here are the rules. Follow them. If you do, we will get along just fine.

A. Arrive on Time

Arrive to class on time. Your professor will be on time. Your professors will expect the same from you. Class starts at 9:00 a.m., not 9:01 a.m.

Lawyers must arrive on time for client meetings, for court appearances, for meetings with partners. If you arrive late you lose clients, you lose cases, you get admonished by judges, and you get fired. Law school is expensive. Do not waste your money or your professor's time.

A few of you are smarter than you look. Get to class 15 minutes early. Settle in, get organized, and review the materials. Sit near the front of the classroom so that you can easily hear and see what's happening. Those who arrive early will have a better chance of doing well. Your professor will notice who comes to class early.

B. Be Prepared

Come to class prepared. Read the assigned reading, have notes on the assigned reading, have briefed the relevant cases, have thought about the reading, and be ready to participate in class discussions. If you are not prepared, you will be lost — class will be pointless. Preparation is not optional if you wish to succeed.

No excuse exists for not being prepared. Never tell your professor you didn't do the reading because you were too busy. Worse yet, never say that you didn't do the reading because you were studying for another class. You are setting up your professional reputation now. You will be judged by your professor and your classmates based on how well prepared you are for class each day. Always come prepared.

C. Attend Every Class

You will attend every class. It may be the school's policy that you must attend at least 90% of all scheduled classes or you will be administratively withdrawn. If you want to pass your courses, attend every class.

There are narrow exceptions to this rule. When I say narrow, I mean narrow: a sudden death in the family or a car accident on the way to school. Traffic is not an excuse. Too many beers the night before is not an excuse. Not wanting to disrupt the class by walking in late is not an excuse.

Sometimes missing class is unavoidable. If it happens, get notes from a fellow student. Never ask your professor if you can meet to go over what you missed. Most professors are happy to answer any questions you have about the material after you review notes from a friend. Most are not willing to repeat an entire lecture to you individually because you missed a class.

D. Engage With Class

During the class period, focus on the class and only the class. Engaging with class means being willing to participate. Learn to enjoy being called on in class. It is an opportunity to learn — the reason you are in law school. Your professor's questions will be tough. It is not expected that you know every answer or even most of them. You may find the questions mystifying. Don't worry. That's okay. That's normal. It will get better as the year progresses.

When asked a question, never "pass." Passing means that either you are unprepared or that you are unwilling to try. Both are unacceptable. Try passing and the questions will only get worse. Help the class avoid the awkward silence while the professor waits for you analyze the case for the first time in class.

You may learn that volunteering when you are prepared is better than waiting for the professor to call on you. Your professors are not stupid.

They know this trick. However, if you have talked recently in class, the professor is more likely to call on someone else. So be proactive. Volunteer when you can. Don't flail, just raise your hand.

E. Answer as a Lawyer Would

In class use plain, easy-to-understand language. Answer in a clear way — not "the party in the first part filed a writ of attachment against the party in the second part, *inter alia*, for failing to construct the structure in which the aforementioned plaintiff resided." That's gibberish. Avoid gibberish even if that's what the judge wrote in the opinion. Your job is to translate what the case has said into plain language.

When your professor asks you to state the facts of a case, do not read verbatim from your casebook. You need to have thought about the case ahead of time so that you can state, in a succinct way, what happened, for what reason, and why.

F. Go to Office Hours

At times you may not understand something discussed in class. That is okay. It is expected. If, after preparing carefully for and attending class you still do not understand, see your professor in office hours. Do not wait until the end of the semester, go soon after the class. This rule is important. Few students go to office hours, but you've paid good money to have access to your professors. Take advantage of it.

There is another reason to visit office hours (even if you understand the material being covered). At some point, you will need to ask your professors for a favor. You may need a letter of recommendation, would like a professor to serve as a job reference, or would like to work as a research assistant. You may need one of your professors to call a judge to get you an interview for a coveted clerkship. Your professors will generally only help and write letters for students they know. If you do not go to office hours, your professors will not know you. Just getting a good grade in class is not enough to get a professor to write a letter of recommendation for you.

G. Ask Only Appropriate Questions

Ask only appropriate questions. Students regularly ask three types of questions in law school: (1) questions designed to make the professor look stupid; (2) questions designed only to make the student look smart; and (3) all other questions. Only ask type #3 questions.

If you ask inappropriate questions, your professor will not be happy. Do not be afraid to ask questions about the material covered in class. It shows you are engaged. It shows you care. It shows you are there to learn. It shows you understand what law school is all about.

H. Be Supportive, Not Competitive

Be supportive of your classmates. Law students do best when they are supportive, not when they are competitive. Share your class notes and your outlines. In the long run, you will be rewarded for your niceness. Your classmates will be your future colleagues. You are building (or destroying) your professional reputation. When a classmate has been called upon, do not roll your eyes, guffaw, or giggle. Listen carefully. They are trying hard. You could be next.

I. Take Responsibility

This may be the most important rule. Take responsibility for your life. If you do not understand everything right away that's fine. That is the way law school works. Work hard and figure it out.

It is not your professor's job to spoon-feed students the law. You must learn the law yourself. Your professor's job is to explore the law's implications, to discuss policy, to ask the hard questions, and to make you think. Law school is an intellectual endeavor. Be introspective. Think and challenge yourself.

A final point. I don't require excessive formality, but I am not John or Julia, I am not "buddy," I'm not "yo, over here." That may sound elitist. Perhaps it is elitist, but that is also the way it is. Once you graduate, I hope we will be on a first-name basis. But that is after you graduate. Right now, let's use "Professor."

––––––––––––

Following these rules is your obligation. A professor never forgets. I expect much from you, and I will show disappointment when my expectations are not met. If you act professionally, I will remember you. I will treat you as an equal. I will do my best to help you succeed. I will consider you for research or teaching assistant positions. I will serve as a reference.

I will write you recommendations. I will follow your career with interest. I will be an eager mentor. Years from now — when you are applying to be a judge, or seeking a partnership, or going for a promotion — I will do what I can to help. I like seeing students succeed. It makes me feel good about life. It keeps me young. It is why I like my job.

Checklist Reminders

Class Reminders

- ❑ *Attend every class and arrive on time (arrive early!)*
- ❑ *Arrive prepared (bring brief, notes, casebook, statutory supplement, pens, pencils, etc.)*
- ❑ *Don't be afraid to participate*
- ❑ *Ask questions when needed (but no showing off!)*
- ❑ *Go to office hours when needed*
- ❑ *Stay engaged and pay attention — listen and think*

3

BRIEFING CASES

One of the skills you will master your first year in law school is how to brief a case. For all your first-year courses, you will be assigned a casebook. Casebooks contain edited portions of judicial decisions (i.e., cases). In class, professors will grill you on what those cases mean. Each case represents one small rule in a larger body of law. By constructing how that small rule relates to the law generally, you learn not only the law but also the process of legal reasoning.

A case brief is a way to be prepared for that grilling, but briefing the cases you read is important for another reason. It teaches you how to read the assigned cases critically, by breaking the case into its component parts. The class discussion of a case goes something like this:

"Mr. James, please tell us the facts of *Perez v. Van Groningen*."

"Well, the court held…," Mr. James sputters only a few words before I cut him off.

"No. I want the facts. Not the holding. I want the facts," I say calmly.

Mr. James gives it another attempt. "Okay. Is it that the court said the employer was liable when a passenger fell from a tractor because the driver was acting within the scope of employment?"

"Ms. Nguyen, please help Mr. James. What are the facts of this case? I want only the facts."

Ms. Nguyen gives it her best shot. "Oh, um, in *Perez*, the plaintiff appealed from a judgment entered on a jury verdict in favor of defendant."

"No. Not procedure. Facts. Just facts."

She replies, "Oh. Um. Perez was living with his uncle. Another one of his uncles, Eulalio Garcia had been told to disk the defendant's orchard. Disking is the process of driving a tractor through an orchard pulling a disking attachment..."

I walk slowly towards Ms. Nguyen and ask, "Where is your case brief?"

I look at her brief on her laptop. There are least eight or nine pages of meticulously prepared notes on *Perez.*

I step away. "Ms. Nguyen, I need a brief. A brief is short — one or two pages at most. Not a book. Not a treatise. But a brief."

"Enough. Close your books. I can see I need to teach you how to prepare for class. I will explain how to brief a case. This may be the most important hour of class you will have all year. Pay attention."

The Basics

Let's start with the basics, and how and why you will write case briefs.

A. A Case Brief Defined

What is a case brief? As its name suggests, it is a short summary of the different components of the cases you read. A brief is nothing more than a study tool: a set of notes, organized in a specific, methodical way, to identify what the case is about and why it was decided in a particular way. A case brief is usually no more than one page long.

Be careful not to be confused. Lawyers also use the term "brief" to refer to a legal memorandum filed in court in support of a motion or an appeal that presents a legal argument. That sort of brief is formal. Formal legal briefs are used to persuade a court to do something. You will learn about formal legal briefs in your first-year legal writing course. That is not the type of brief I am talking about.

The brief I will describe below is a case brief. It is a tool law students use to prepare for each of the cases you are assigned to read in law school. It is a means of analyzing the cases and preparing for the questions you will be asked by your professor.

B. Why You Will Brief

A case brief is useful for several reasons. It will help you understand the material, prepare for class, and complete an outline. Rewriting and summarizing material leads to better comprehension. Perhaps most importantly, a brief helps you distill a case down to its important parts. Doing so allows you to understand and remember key components of a case — particularly helpful when you are being called on in class.

Cases have a unique structure and method to them that is different from other kinds of writing. When you first begin law school, you will find cases difficult to read and understand. Briefing a case calls upon your analytical reading ability. By breaking down the different components of the case, you train yourself to read and understand cases more quickly. This is important. By dissecting a case into its component parts, you improve your legal analysis and legal reasoning skills.

Upper division students will often give you bad advice. They will tell you that briefing takes too much time; that briefing does not help you do well on your exams; that briefing is not essential to class preparation. Ignore them. Of course, some students may do well on exams without briefing, but you are not briefing solely to prepare for the exam, and, more importantly, you will not know if you are one of those students who can do well without briefing until it's too late.

C. How to Use Your Case Brief

Keep your case brief accessible during class. Take notes on it as the professor discusses the case. By the end of class, the case brief should be covered with additional notes and jottings spurred by the day's class discussion. In using a printed copy, consider using oversized margins so you will have plenty of space to make annotations.

At the end of the week, you should review your briefs and take the information you've learned and place it in a course outline. You should synthesize the week's material into an outline and use your case briefs as a starting point for doing that. We'll talk more about outlining later.

How to Read Cases

To brief a case properly, you must first be able to read and understand the case. The difficulty is that reading in law school is different from reading in college. In college, the reading was generally straightforward and descriptive. Reading cases in law school is not like reading a textbook in college. Nor is it like reading a novel.

A. Prepare to Read

Give some thought to your environment. You need a place with no distractions, where you can read without interruptions. You cannot read law school cases with the necessary focus with the TV on, while you're doing laundry, while you're on the bus. You need a quiet, distraction-free environment. Be honest with yourself. If reading in a nice, comfy chair will lead to an inevitable nap, get a stiff, hard-back chair. If reading in the library will lead to socializing, go somewhere else.

B. Preview the Case

Previewing a case is an important first step to reading. Before you start reading the case, get a sense of where it fits into the class generally. What is the context? Where does the case fit in the casebook's table of contents or the course syllabus? What is the case likely to be about, and why is the professor assigning it now? Are you able to get an idea as to the key issues the case will be about and where it fits into the course? Placing the case in the broader context will give you a framework to work with and make the case easier to read and understand.

Let's take an example. Assume your assignment for class is to read *R v. Dudley and Stephens*. Before reading the case, look to your syllabus or textbook and see which legal topic the case falls within. If you look to your class syllabus, you may see that you will be covering "necessity" in the next class and that necessity falls under the broader topic of "murder." You now know the topic on which to focus as you read. Although the case may discuss other issues in addition to the topic of necessity, you know to read it for the purpose of understanding when a party acts out of necessity. Knowing why you are reading the case before you read it makes the case easier to understand. You can also use your class syllabus to place the rules you learn from the cases in a broader context. If your syllabus includes the *R v. Dudley and Stephens* case under the topic "Defenses to Murder," you can start to piece together the bigger picture that necessity is a defense to murder. A professor's syllabus is a great tool to help you in briefing cases and will also be helpful when you start outlining for the course.

C. Read Carefully

After you've placed the case in context, you should read the case carefully all the way through. Do not skim. Judicial opinions are too complicated to understand from a cursory review. You must pay attention to detail. If a sentence or a paragraph does not make sense, stop and re-read. Don't move on until you understand what you have read.

When reading a case, it is not enough to understand what the judge writing the opinion has said. You must understand why the judges chose to reach the specific decision. Students should energetically attack the case and assess what is written. Is what the judge said correct? You may be surprised to know that judges are not always right. They misread the law. They misunderstand the law. They have flawed logic. Critically assess the judge's decision. What follows from the holding? How does the decision compare to other decisions? Is the case merely applying a prior rule, or creating a new one? Why is the case in the casebook? You will likely need to read each case two or three times to have a deep understanding of the issues.

D. Use a Legal Dictionary

When you begin law school, you are as much learning a new language as you are learning the law. You must look up words you do not understand. If a case in your property textbook refers to a "conveyance" and you don't know what that means, look it up. Professors do not have time during class to teach legal terminology. They will expect that you know the definition of every word found in the case. Even words you think you know might have a particular, if not peculiar, legal meaning. You will be tempted to gloss over words, but don't. Building your legal vocabulary is an important skill. Most of the cases that you read will be chock full of archaic terms, Latinisms, or other legalese. You may come across hundreds of new terms in the first weeks of law school. If you fail to look those terms up, you will be at a disadvantage. Professors often ask students in class what those terms mean.

E. Avoid Excessive Highlighting

When reading the case for the first time, avoid excessive highlighting. Highlighting can be useful for many students, but you should employ highlighting cautiously. As students are often unsure on what details to focus, many students end up with a book filled with yellow. That makes highlighting useless. Students who use highlighters excessively also have a tendency to skim the words they are highlighting. The same is true for excessive underlining. The first time you read a case, read it through carefully and then go back and highlight or underline details you find particularly important.

F. Take Selective Notes

Just as you should be nervous about excessive highlighting, also be wary of taking too many notes (at least the first time you're reading the case). Taking some notes will keep you engaged and reading actively. You do not have time, however, to write essays on every case you read. Avoid filling the margins of your casebook with mindless jottings. Save the writing for when you write the case brief.

G. Keep Track of the Parties

When reading a court decision, you should keep track of the parties. In civil cases, you have a plaintiff and a defendant. The plaintiff is asserting the claim and seeking a remedy. In a criminal case, you have the government (state or federal) and the defendant.

The name of the party initiating the court action, no matter at what stage of the judicial proceedings, appears first in the legal papers. For example, if Jones sued Smith in Federal District Court (i.e., the trial court), Jones is the plaintiff and the case is known as *Jones v. Smith*. If Jones loses in the District Court, she may appeal. At that time, in the Court of Appeals, Jones (the appealing party) is referred to as the appellant and Smith becomes the appellee. The case is still known as *Jones v. Smith*. If Jones then wins on appeal and Smith successfully petitions the U.S. Supreme Court to hear the case, the name of the case will change to *Smith v. Jones*. Smith is now the petitioner and Jones is the respondent. Changes to case titles are common in criminal cases because most reach the appellate courts when a convicted defendant appeals.

H. Distinguish Kinds of Opinions

As you read, be careful to distinguish the kind of opinion you are reading. What court is deciding the case? Is it a federal or a state court? Is it a trial or an appellate court? Is this a majority, dissenting, concurring, or plurality opinion?

A majority opinion is an opinion that is agreed to by the court's majority (for the U.S. Supreme Court, usually five of nine justices). A concurring opinion agrees with the majority's disposition of the case but is written to express a particular judge's reasoning. A dissenting opinion, in contrast, disagrees with the majority's disposition and will set out the dissenting judge's reasons for disagreeing. Lastly, a plurality opinion is the opinion from a group of justices in a case where no single opinion received support from a sufficient number of justices to create a majority.

How to Brief

No one formula exists for what should be included in a case brief. The contents of a brief should vary depending on the course and the professor. However, certain components are common to all briefs: the issue, the facts, the procedure, the holding, the rules, and the court's reasoning. I am going to take you through each of these parts and explain how they work.

A. The Issue

In this section you want to identify what legal issue the court is deciding. You will be reading cases that have been appealed to a higher court. An appellate court hears a case on appeal when one of the parties believes there is a problem with the lower court's decision. You must identify the problem at issue between the parties. A well-written court decision will often begin by setting out the legal issue. Even if the court sets forth the issue, take the time to carefully phrase the issue in your own words. Do not blindly follow the wording of the court.

You can state the issue in many ways, but a strong issue statement will include (i) the legal principle at issue and (ii) the significant facts relevant to that legal principle. Conventionally, the issue is a short, single-sentence question. If framed properly, the question will be able to be answered with a "yes" or "no." The question should be objective and not slanted in favor of one party. A common way of framing a legal issue is to use the format: "Under... does... when...." It works like this: Under [state the jurisdiction], does [state the particular legal issue] when [state the legally relevant facts].

Let's consider an example taken from a California Supreme Court case, *Perez v. Van Groningen*. In *Perez*, an employee was driving a tractor to disk his employer's orchards. The employer had previously told the driver that no passengers were permitted to ride on the tractor. However, on one occasion the employee allowed his nephew to ride along. The nephew fell off the tractor and was injured. The nephew sued the driver's employer for damages, but could only prevail if the injury occurred within the driver's scope of employment.

A good issue statement might read: "<u>Under</u> California law, <u>does</u> an employee act within the scope of employment <u>when</u> he takes an unauthorized passenger with him in performing duties assigned by his employer?" This issue statement is effective because it includes not just the specific legal issue before the court (scope of employment), but identifies the relevant facts as well. It is specific enough to identify what is going on in the case, yet broad enough to be applied in future cases as well.

An issue statement that included only "Was the employee acting within the scope of employment?" is abstract and omits the facts that bring to life what occurred in the case to place it in context. There are hundreds of cases about whether an employee is acting within the scope of employment and, without further information, one would not know enough to determine what the case is about. The issue is too broad to be helpful to anyone. It needs more detail.

An issue statement can, however, be too specific. For example, the following issue statement includes too many details: "Is a tractor driver acting within the scope of employment when he is asked to disk the orchards of his employer and takes his nephew along with him without his employer's permission?" This issue statement may be technically correct; however, the purpose of reading cases is to use them to predict how courts will decide future cases. It is unlikely that future cases you encounter will be about tractor drivers, nephews, and disking orchards. Moreover, some of these facts — such as the relationship of the driver and the passenger — are not material to the court's decision.

Remember, more than one "right" issue statement exists. As long as your issue statement marries relevant facts and legal principles, and is clear and concise, you may word it in different ways.

B. The Facts

You should summarize the legally significant facts of the case. What happened? What gave rise to the lawsuit? What is this case all about? Do not cut and paste what is contained in the case itself. Instead, simplify. Who sued who for what? What was the crime? What happened that gave rise to the lawsuit?

The facts section should be short: one (maybe two) paragraphs. Only include those facts necessary to understand the case. This is difficult, but struggling to identify the facts that are key to the court's decision is important. If you understand what facts were crucial to the court's decision, you likely understand the case. Another small point: use descriptive terms rather than proper names when referring to parties. It is usually more helpful to refer to the parties as the buyer, seller, driver, passenger, employer, employee, etc., than Smith, Jones, Perez, etc. Once you decide how to refer to the parties, be consistent throughout your brief.

Let's return to our example of the injured passenger. The brief's facts section would include: (i) the defendant employed the driver; (ii) the driver's regular duties included disking the orchard; (iii) a passenger rode with the driver; (iv) passengers were not permitted on the tractor; and (v) the passenger was injured. That's it. Keep your facts section short.

Much of the factual description set forth in the cases you read will not be relevant to the issue before the court. For example, whether the injured passenger lived with his uncle is not relevant to whether the driver was acting within the scope of his employment. Similarly, what orchard disking is, where the passenger was sitting in the tractor, and whether the passenger had a broken bone or a concussion are all irrelevant to the case's holding. Interesting facts, maybe, but not legally significant to whether the driver was acting within the scope of employment. Sometimes you may wish to include one or two descriptive facts to provide context; however, including too many descriptive facts will result in a case brief as long as the case itself and distract from the facts that really matter. If a fact is not legally significant, leave it out.

In determining which facts are the most relevant, it is helpful to look to the reasoning of the court and see what facts the court relied on to reach its decision.

C. The Procedure

Not only should you explain what gave rise to the lawsuit, you should also briefly explain how the case came before the appellate court. Understanding the stages the case went through before reaching the appellate court will help put the case in context and understand the issues. So summarize what happened in the lower court. Identify the courts that have made rulings in the case and how those rulings have led to the appeal. For example, in a criminal case, was the defendant convicted? Was there a trial? In a civil case, was the defendant found liable? Was there a trial? Did a party file a motion? What kind of motion? How did the lower court rule? Who appealed?

In our tractor-injury example, the passenger filed suit against the employer. There was a jury trial and the jury returned a verdict in the employer's favor. The passenger appealed arguing that the court should have instructed the jury that the driver was acting within the scope of employment. These are the procedural facts. They are not what actually happened to cause the injury, but what happened in court after the plaintiff filed suit.

D. The Rules

In an appeal, a court will apply particular rules of law to reach its result. For the rules section of your brief, you need to determine what rule or legal principles the court applied. Sometimes rules are directly taken from a statute or code (passed by the legislature). Sometimes the rules are judge-made law created from prior case law.

Often there are several different rules in one case. A court often addresses many different issues in each case and each issue will have its own rules. Even if there is only one issue before the court, the case will often set forth multiple rules related to that one issue. A court may even set forth the same rule multiple times but use a variety of different ways of saying the same thing. Your job is to identify all the rules that apply to the specific issue you are working on for class. Next, combine those relevant rules into one concise rule statement that can be inserted into your brief. It is often helpful to paraphrase the legal rule rather than merely copying it verbatim. However, if the rules are simple and straightforward, you can include them exactly as the court has stated them.

Let's use our tractor example to illustrate. In determining whether the tractor driver was acting within the scope of his employment, the court set forth several different legal rules, including the following statements:

- An employer is liable for risks arising out of employment.
- A risk arises out of employment when an employee's conduct is <u>not so unusual or startling</u> that it would seem unfair to include the loss as a cost of business.
- An employer is liable for an employee's actions if the risk was <u>typical given the enterprise undertaken</u>.
- An employee's actions are unusual if the employee substantially deviated from the duties assigned to further the employee's own personal ends.

What should you do with these different rules about scope of employment? You need to take these rules and devise a rule summary for when an employer will be liable for acts of an employee. Start with the general rule that an employer is liable for risks arising out of employment. However, this rule alone is insufficient. You need to describe when a risk "arises out of employment." You can see from the rules above that risks arise out of one's employment if they are "not so unusual or startling." The rules also include that a defendant is liable if the risk was "typical given the enterprise." Both of these rules pretty much say the same thing. You don't need to include both. Choose one or the other or synthesize them into one idea. Then add the rule about "substantial deviation" to your rule statement. The idea about "substantial deviation" is different from the previous two rules. It is more specific. It tells you when something is considered atypical or unusual. It should be added as a third sentence to your rule summary.

So your rule section might state: "An employer is liable for risks arising out of employment. Risks arising out of employment include risks that are typical given the enterprise undertaken. However, an employer will not be liable for an employee's negligent acts when the employee substantially deviates from the duties assigned."

Keep in mind, this is just one acceptable way of phrasing the rule. Many other versions would also be correct. Just remember to include enough of the rule to understand how to apply it and remember to combine like parts together so you don't have a rule that is a page long listing every detail the court mentioned. Taking the time to fit the different legal rules together will help you master the case and have you ready when your name is called out in class.

E. The Holding

Your brief should also precisely state the decision's holding. What did the court do? What was the outcome? For which side did the court rule? The holding should be one sentence that provides the court's decision on the specific issue before it. If the *Perez* court ruled for the injured passenger who fell off of the tractor, the holding of the court would be that the driver was acting within the scope of his employment.

Do not confuse the court's holding with the court's disposition of the case. The disposition is the action a court takes as a result of its holding. Perhaps the court affirmed the lower court's decision. Perhaps the court reversed the lower court's decision. Perhaps the court remanded the decision for further action. These actions are called the "disposition." Some professors confuse the terminology. A professor may call the court's action to reverse the decision a "holding." That is incorrect; however, I do not recommend you bring this to your professor's attention. You must adjust to your professor's terminology and follow your professor's specific instructions for his or her class. Technically, however, a holding is the court's answer to the legal question. If the issue is whether an employee acted within the scope of employment, the holding is either the employee acted within the scope of employment or the employee did not act within the scope of employment. The disposition is the action the court takes as a result of that holding (affirmed, reversed, remanded).

F. The Reasoning

In appellate decisions, the judge will explain why he or she reached a particular decision. In the reasoning section of your case brief, you should summarize the reasoning behind the court's decision.

In *Perez*, the court held the employer was acting within the scope of employment. Why did the court make that decision? Assume the court explained that the driver was engaged in work activities at the time of the incident and falling out of a tractor was a typical risk that comes with disking orchards. Perhaps the court also explained that the lack of authorization to take a passengers was irrelevant because it is not necessary to show actions are authorized in order for employee to be acting within scope of employment. If these are the reasons given by the court, include them in the "reasoning" section of your case brief. Include both reasons. Students have a tendency to find one relevant reason for the court's holding and move on. Your job is to completely understand the court's reasons. Keep your summary brief, but include all relevant reasons offered by the court.

One more tip. If the court uses policy as part of the reasoning, make sure to note the policy as well. Policy is the reason why a legal rule exists in the first place. Professors love policy. They love to ask law students about policy. They love to challenge students to consider whether the policy for a particular rule is rational. Always note any policy considerations by the court as part of your reasoning.

An example of a case and its corresponding case brief can be found in Appendix B. Use the example to get a good feel for what a case brief should look like before jumping into drafting case briefs for your own classes.

Avoiding Pitfalls

There are a few pitfalls to avoid when briefing a case.

A. Do Not "Book Brief"

Book briefing is when you only take notes in the margins of your casebook. That's fine as a complement, but not as a substitute for a case brief. You should have a separate document that forces you to think about and write out the different components of the court's decision. The same is true with "highlighter briefing" where students use different color highlighters to distinguish the different parts of the case. If you like your book to look like a rainbow, that's fine, but again, it complements and should not replace a case brief. Writing out and synthesizing what you've read is an important skill to develop.

B. Value Substance Over Style

Do not spend hours making your brief look pretty. This is not a beauty contest. A case brief is a learning tool. It should not be treated as a sacrosanct document. Of course, it should be nicely set out in a useable and easy to read format, but don't spend hours tinkering with how it looks. Substance is more important here. You don't get extra points for having a really nice looking brief that says nothing.

C. Do Not Cut and Paste

Some students have a nasty habit of looking up the case online and then cutting and pasting large portions of the case's language (or worse yet, just mindlessly typing what the case says verbatim) into the case brief. Don't. A case brief is intended to force you to carefully read and analyze a case. One of the primary goals in law school is for you to teach yourself how to read complicated cases and understand the law. If you simply retype what the judge has said, you are doing an end-run around a key reason for case briefing. Cutting and pasting your brief will also not prepare you for the professor's questions during class. Professors want students to answer questions in their *own* words. If you quote the case verbatim, your professor's next question will be, "Great, can you summarize that in your own words?" If you have already summarized the case in your words for your case brief, it will be much easier to respond the professor's question.

D. Do Not Use a Commercial Brief

Do not use commercial outlines or commercial case summaries when briefing. These materials can be useful to help you understand the material you are covering, but they are not a replacement for working (perhaps struggling) with the material and briefing the case yourself. Remember the purpose of briefing: to help you to understand the different components of a case and read critically. Using a commercial outline or case summary defeats (or at least undermines) that purpose.

That's all. Next time I expect you to be prepared for my questions. Unless you brief, you won't be. I trust I won't have to repeat myself. I'm done for today. Next class we'll pick up where we left off and Mr. James can tell us the facts of the *Perez* case.

Checklist Reminders

Reading Cases

- ❏ _Find a quiet, distraction-free place to read_
- ❏ _Preview the case (skim it!)_
- ❏ _Read carefully and critically_
- ❏ _Look up terms you are unfamiliar with_
- ❏ _Take selective notes and avoid excessive highlighting_
- ❏ _Keep track of the parties (who is the plaintiff, who is the defendant)_
- ❏ _Focus on what court is deciding the issue (trial or appellate, state or federal, etc.)_

To Remember When Briefing

- ❏ _Use a standard, easy-to-read format_
- ❏ _Include at least: (1) a statement of issues, (2) facts, (3) procedure, (4) rules, (5) holding, and (6) reasoning_
- ❏ _Keep the brief short — one page or less ideally_
- ❏ _Don't book brief_
- ❏ _Don't cut and paste (must think about what you are writing)_
- ❏ _Don't use a commercial brief_
- ❏ _Annotate and make notes on the brief during class_
- ❏ _Tailor brief for class preparation and individual professor_

4

OUTLINING

––––––––––

Class had only just begun when a student raised his hand and asked what sounded like an innocuous question. "Professor, we've read a number of cases, but I don't see how they tie together. I was speaking with some of my classmates. It would be really helpful if you could explain how they connect together and give us the big picture."

I paused and took a deep breath. "I'm sure it would be helpful. It would probably be helpful if I wrote the exam for you too! I am not doing the work for you. Welcome to the real world. But I will explain how YOU can tie it all together. Close your books. This morning I will explain how to outline."

The Basics

Many students underestimate how important outlining is in law school. Before explaining how to outline, let me explain why you should outline, when you should begin outlining, and what you will be outlining. I'll finish by emphasizing a few things you should avoid.

A. Why You Will Outline

You will outline because it is the process of outlining that matters. Outlining is not about the finished product. The process of outlining forces you to organize, synthesize, and understand more fully the different topics and issues you have covered in class. Outlining — done correctly — gives you a roadmap or a strategy for tackling exam questions and requires you to think methodically about the material you have covered. By struggling with the material to create an outline and then working with that outline, you will understand the material better and will be able to see the "big picture." After outlining, you should be able to identify the overarching concepts around which the course revolved and the significant legal principles relevant to those concepts. Law school outlines are also necessary because skimming over all the material you have covered in a semester is impossible. You need some condensed way to review the material for the exam. In short, outlines are study aids.

It is foolish to borrow an outline from another student or download an outline from an "outline bank" on the internet. It is foolish to solely rely on commercial outlines. Commercial outlines serve their purpose — just a different purpose from the one you might expect. Commercial outlines may provide an overview at the start of a law school course — sort of a preview of things to come to help you see the forest from the trees. You can also use a commercial outline when you get stuck — to help you understand the material in a way that makes sense to you. Commercial outlines can sometimes help you organize your thoughts if you are confused as to an area of the law, but they are supplements, and supplements only. They can never replace the process of creating your own outline. Doing it yourself allows you to organize, learn, and think through the material you must know for the final exam.

B. When to Outline

You should begin outlining early. Many students will wait until the end of the semester, just before exams to start. You should not. In your first year of law school, you should start no later than the fourth or fifth week of a fifteen-week semester. You have likely not covered sufficient material to start any earlier than this. Courses in the first year usually start out slowly. After the first semester of law school, you should begin outlining in the second or third week of the semester.

Starting early is important. You cannot possibly start and finish everything you need to do in the last few weeks of the semester. In addition to outlining, you will need to complete practice exams, memorize key rules, and review the material the professors have covered. Students who wait until late in the semester to begin outlining are almost guaranteeing themselves a lower grade. Outlining early is also important because the more you go over the material, the more likely you will understand it in a meaningful way.

You should create a schedule. In that schedule, set aside time each week to outline your different courses. Some students set aside Saturday or Sunday solely for outlining. Others prefer to read on the weekend and carve out a different evening of the week to outline for each course. Either way is fine. The key is to create a schedule and stick with it and update your outline each week. If you do not, getting sidetracked is easy.

C. When to Stop Outlining

When should you finish your outline? Plan to complete your outline on the last day of class (or the weekend following the last day of class). You do not want to be outlining right up to the exam. Too many students wait too long and use up precious time right before the exam that should be used to learn the material. Outlining is a process. It helps you understand the material discussed in class. If you've kept to your schedule and updated your outline each week, you should finish just as the course is finishing.

D. What to Outline

In law school, you will find students with massive outlines—hundreds upon hundreds of pages of material containing everything one could possibly want to know about the course's subject matter. These massive tombs will contain the student's class notes, the student's notes on the reading, the student's notes on their notes, the student's summary of commercial outlines, the student's notes on hornbooks, their notes from study group meetings, excerpts from statutes, excerpts from cases, hypothetical questions from class, and maybe even the professors musing and ramblings on various topics. These kinds of War-and-Peace outlines make students feel warm and comfy knowing that they have transcribed everything anyone could ever want to know about a topic. The outline's author will be proud — and it will be absolutely and completely useless.

A good outline is not an "information dump." You are not writing a treatise when you outline. Instead, an outline should be a condensed, focused, summary of the key legal rules on a topic. An outline is a step-by-step guide on what is needed to win under the law. Legal rules are like a recipe. Legal rules have ingredients. The different ingredients are called "elements." Plaintiffs have to prove "elements" of the law to win the case. You need to organize your outline by these elements/ingredients.

An illustration may make this easier to follow. If you were to read a book about Italian baking, you might start with the history of baking in Venice, how Italian tastes changed over time, the major influences on Italian food, the different signature dishes of Italian deserts, etc. Yet if you want to make an Italian cake, the history of baking in Venice and how it has changed over time is irrelevant. You just need the recipe and steps that must be taken to make the cake. You must know you need to buy sugar, flour, and eggs. You must know to put the sugar and flour in the bowl before the eggs and in what amount. It is of little help to know that the first cake was baked in 1300 B.C.

The same logic applies to your law school courses. In class and in the readings you will likely explore the legal history of a law, the policy implications behind a law, as well as many other interesting topics. However, for your law school exams, all you need is a step-by-step recipe on how to prove a legal rule. You need to know the elements or ingredients of the rule. Let's take a legal example. Assume your client was assaulted and you are arguing the case in front of the jury. To win the case, you need to prove all the elements of an assault. The defendant must have:

1. Voluntarily acted;
2. Intended to create apprehension of imminent harmful or offensive contact; and
3. Caused reasonable apprehension of imminent harmful or offensive conduct.

There are three "ingredients" to an assault. Organize your outline around these three ingredients. You do not need to include the history of assault or how the assault developed over time. The history of assault is not relevant to whether you can win your case. Even if your professor discusses the history of assault in class, it is not likely to be tested on the exam. Law school exams focus on the elements of each legal claim. Law school exams ask the student to apply the elements of the law to a set of facts. Organize your outline accordingly.

You will also want to briefly mention policy or include brief examples from the cases you read, but the policy and examples should be relatively short. The outline should primarily be focused on the elements of each legal rule. Simply list the ingredients.

E. What to Avoid

A few things to avoid when outlining. As an initial matter, do not get bogged down with case names and minute details of cases. Most professors do not require that sort of detail. The goal of law school is not to have you memorize thousands of inconsequential, nit-picky facts. Instead, you need to know the elements of the rules. An outline necessarily removes legal nuances and fact-specific distinctions in cases and forces you to think of general legal principles.

Do not get hung up with formatting. An outline is a tool for you to understand the material. Sure, it must be organized. It should be readable and easy for you to follow. But you are not making a holy manuscript. Do not spend tons of time getting the fonts, and the colors, and the bolding just right. That's not the point.

Lastly, do not cut-and-paste large swaths of text from your notes or from cases. Remember, outlining is a process. It requires you to think. By thinking you will learn the material and understand it better.

How to Outline

Drafting an outline takes several steps. Here are some basic suggestions for creating one.

A. Get Organized

Before you begin you will want to be organized. Ensure you're in a comfortable place with enough room to stretch out. At minimum, you should have with you: (1) the course syllabus; (2) the course casebook; (3) any course supplement, rule, or code book; (4) your class notes and case briefs; (5) any course materials or handouts; and (6) any supplementary resources you might have to help you understand the material (e.g., hornbooks). When crafting your outline, you will likely need to consult all these sources.

B. Organize around Legal Topics

You want to begin by getting a sense of the big picture. You should organize your outline around concepts and legal topics, not around cases. In class you read cases, but the outline needs to be broader than that. It needs to focus on the main legal issues and principles of law that you studied. In your first-year torts class, for example, you may have read hundreds of cases. Don't list those cases. Instead your torts outline would have headings that set out the main issues you studied, such as assault, battery, false imprisonment, intentional infliction of emotional distress, etc.

There's a fairly easy way to start an outline. Look at your course syllabus and your casebook's table of contents. Look at the main sections that you have covered in class from the table of contents or from the course's syllabus. Write them down. These will be the major sections of your outline. This will ensure that you are organizing your outline by topics and issues rather than by cases.

C. Subdivide into Legal Elements

After you have identified the main topics of the course from the table of contents, course syllabus, or from your class notes, you should subdivide the outline further. You should break each topic down into its main components, and include all the elements for each legal issue. Be sure to flesh out each part or sub-part with a definition or explanation.

When subdividing the main topics into legal elements, keep in mind the relationship between the sub-parts. Are they in the right order? Are they in the right hierarchy? For each legal issue, you should break the rule into elements and identify any exceptions. For example, in torts, you might have studied several different intentional torts, such as assault, battery, false imprisonment, intentional infliction of emotional distress, etc. Each of these topics should be listed as an item on your outline. Within each topic, break down the tort into its elements. List them by number. You should be able to see the number of distinct elements each tort requires. In addition to the elements, make sure to include any exceptions or defenses related to the legal issue. If the exception or the defense applies specifically to one topic, but not the others, list the defense or exception within that topic. However, if the exception or defense applies equally to several legal issues, list the exceptions or defenses after you have listed all relevant legal issues. Here is an example. The example provides a general overview of an outline of intentional torts, with only the elements for assault broken down.

Intentional Torts

I. Battery

II. Assault

    1.   Voluntary act by the defendant

         a.   The defendant took some form of action or conduct.

         b.   Contact is not necessary, but words alone are not enough.

         c.   Case example

    2.   Intent to create apprehension of imminent harmful or offensive contact:

         a.   Intent can be shown if the defendant desired to cause apprehension of harmful/offensive bodily contact or knew with substantial certainty it would occur.

         b.   The defendant's own words can negate intent.

         c.   Case example

    3.   Defendant caused reasonable apprehension of imminent harmful or offensive conduct:

         a.   Fear is not required for apprehension.

         b.   Reasonable apprehension occurs if (i) the plaintiff believes offensive conduct is imminent and (ii) the belief is justified.

         c.   Threats of future harm are not sufficient.

         d.   Case example

III. Intentional Infliction of Emotional Distress

IV. [Additional Intentional Torts]

V. Exceptions to Intentional Torts

VI. Defenses to Intentional Torts

VII. Policy relating to Intentional Torts

Quick note about elements: not every legal issue breaks down into elements. In your property course, for example, you may learn about something called "tracing." Tracing is a concept where one can follow the trail of an asset if an asset is sold and the proceeds of the sale are subsequently put into the bank. There are no elements to prove "tracing." You don't have ingredients to prove tracing exists. Tracing is just a method of following money. If no elements exist, simply list the legal concept in the relevant part of your outline. Legal issues without elements are rare — especially in your first year of law school. Most legal issues have at least one element. Even if there is just one element, organize your outline around that one element. Make sure that one element is the key focus of your outline.

D. Blend In Key Cases and Statutes

After you have identified the main topics and the elements to each legal issue, your next step is to include information about the relevant statutes, codes, or cases you studied. You should blend into your outline the important statutes or cases that relate to each element, as well as include key hypotheticals or illustrations that demonstrate how the elements work.

Cases are examples of how the elements of a rule work in practice. In writing an exam answer, cases can be used as analogies. So be sure to note, very quickly, how the cases you have read demonstrate how the rule applies. When you come to the exam, this exercise will allow you to make arguments by analogy (arguments that support a conclusion through comparing the facts of the problem with the facts of prior court decisions). On the other hand, be careful not to get bogged down in too many details. An outline should not be a compilation of case briefs. Your outline should include only key cases and the summary of the case should generally be no more than 1–2 sentences.

E. Include Policy and Reasoning

For each rule or element, quickly identify any relevant policy behind it. Professors like to talk about policy. Policy is the reason why a law exists. In exams, discussing policy can be the difference between an A and a B. Understanding the policy or reasons behind a particular rule will help you address tough questions in a nuanced, more sophisticated way. If your professor spent a lot of time discussing why is the rule the way it is, briefly include that policy in your outline.

Other Considerations

A few other things are worth keeping in mind as you begin outlining for a course.

A. The Condensed Outline

At some point, you should condense your outline to one or two pages. This should normally be done in the last few weeks before the exam, just as the course is ending. This very short outline serves as a checklist for the key points in the course. You should memorize this condensed outline to ensure that you spot the issues being tested and have a framework for attack.

You want to think of this as the step-by-step guide to the course and to answering an exam question. So usually the condensed outline is limited to the elements of the different legal rules you have studied. You should remove the cases and the examples that were contained in the longer outline. The longer outline helps you learn and synthesize the course material. The condensed outline is solely to give you something manageable to study while going into the exam.

B. It's a Personal Thing

Outlines can look very different. Don't worry if your outline is not as pretty as your friend's, or doesn't contain the exact same information. An outline is a tool that helps you understand and organize the material covered in class. What works for you might not work for someone else. This is another reason why you want to create your own outline, rather than simply copy someone else's. While your outline must be complete, the length of an outline has little correlation to quality.

C. Flowcharts

Some students are visual learners. If you are, you might consider creating a flow chart for each course. Flow charts are a different way of organizing the many rules you must learn and understanding the relationship between those rules. Just like an outline, a flow chart can provide you with a plan of attack — a step-by-step approach — to analyzing a particular question. An outline may be more complicated than a flowchart and permits you to organize a large amount of material. Creating a flowchart forces you to think carefully about the different steps required in analyzing a particular area of law.

D. Open and Closed Book Exams

Some will tell you that an outline for a closed-book exam should look substantially different than an outline for an open-book exam (i.e., an exam where you may consult your notes and outline during the exam). Don't believe them. As a preliminary matter, whether you may bring an outline into the exam or not, the outline must be organized and structured in a way that you can synthesize and understand the material covered. An outline's primary purpose remains as a tool for learning the material, regardless of the style of exam given. More importantly, the "open" part of an open-book exam is often misleading. Usually even in an open book exam you must know the material by heart — you do not time to consult your outline or notes.

There may be some slight differences between how you outline for a closed-book exam as compared to an open-book exam. One difference may be the condensed outline. Generally a condensed outline, which contains just key concepts and rules, is more important for closed book exams where you must memorize the outline. Another difference may be the use of colors and tabs. In an open-book exam, some professors suggest coloring and tabbing your outline so that you can look things up more quickly during the exam (e.g., a different colored tab for each topic, and different colored ink for key rules).

That's it. That is how you will learn to take what is discussed in class and see how it all relates together. By outlining you will prepare for the final exam and will figure out the big picture yourself. Take the time to look at the sample outline, condensed outline, and flowchart in Appendix C to get a feel for what lies ahead.

Checklist Reminders

The Basics

- ❑ *Start the fourth or fifth week of the semester (first year)*
- ❑ *Create a schedule for updating outlines each week*
- ❑ *Write outline as a roadmap for the final exam*
- ❑ *A study aid — worry about substance more than form*

How to Do It

- ❑ *Get ready (find a quiet place, bring course materials, notes, etc.)*
- ❑ *Organize outline around legal topics (not cases), looking at course syllabus or casebook table of contents for organizational ideas*
- ❑ *Subdivide each topic into their components*
- ❑ *Break each legal rule into its separate elements (write rule summaries)*

- ❑ *Blend in key cases ad statutes— around rules*
- ❑ *Include examples and hypos covered in class*
- ❑ *Note key policy considerations*
- ❑ *Keep it relatively short*

Other Considerations

- ❑ *Create a condensed outline near end of semester (just a few pages) with key rules*
- ❑ *Try working with flowcharts*
- ❑ *Tailor outline depending on whether exam is open or closed book*

STUDYING

Preparing for class means more than pulling the facts and holding from a case. It means more than giving the cases a quick read. You are in law school to learn how to analyze, to question the reasoning in the opinions, and to exercise your own judgment about them. It is hard work, and there is no easy way around it.

Before Class

In preparing for class, remembering the purpose of law school is essential. You are not here just to learn the law. You are here to learn to analyze critically and to think creatively. You must work through issues presented by cases and exercise your own judgment about them. That requires careful preparation and study.

A. Setting a Schedule

Ensuring adequate preparation time for each and every class will require setting a study schedule and sticking with it. Schedule three hours of study time for every hour of class. I do not mean three hours a week for each class you have. I mean three hours each week for every hour you are in class. Thus, if you meet for twelve hours during the week, you will schedule approximately thirty six hours of studying time for the week. (What, you say — that's more than forty hours a week? Heaven forbid. Welcome to real life kiddo!)

During the scheduled study time, you will read and brief cases, prepare for class, prepare your own outlines, review your outlines, and take practice exams. During the first few weeks of law school, just reading and briefing cases will absorb most of your study time. By around the fourth week, it will be time to begin outlining. Reviewing outlines, making flashcards, and taking practice exams will start soon thereafter. Studying for exams cannot wait until finals week. It must be part of your weekly routine.

Some of you will prepare for class during the week (the night before each class) and save the weekend hours for outlining, reviewing, and taking practice exams. Others will finish the entire week's reading over the weekend so you can spend each night after class updating your outlines and taking practice exams. Both strategies are fine. Your approach may vary, but allocate your time between all of these areas and do not wait until dead week to start preparing for exams.

You will be tempted to put work off until the end of the semester. It won't work. This isn't college. Once your schedule is made, you must stick with it. Socializing with your friends does not count toward your scheduled study time each week — even if you are talking about torts while at the local pub.

B. The Right Environment

When studying, ensure you are in a comfortable place without distractions. Ideally you should be in a place where you have enough room to stretch out. Before beginning, think ahead so you have what you need for the next hour. You don't want to be jumping up every few minutes to get a book, or a pen, or another cup of coffee.

C. Before Reading a Case

Often there is an introduction to the case that you may have a hankering to skip. Don't. The introduction will place the case in context and will often indicate the statute or constitutional provision on which the court bases its decision. If the casebook tells you to read Article III of the Constitution or read a Federal Rule of Civil Procedure before reading the case, look it up and read it carefully. If you don't, you likely will understand the case only superficially. If you have a "rule book" or a "statutory supplement" for a course, it should be tired, well-worn and dog-eared by the semester's end.

D. Reading a Case

We have talked previously about how to read a case to write a case brief, but preparing properly involves more than creating a brief. Certainly you need to know the facts, holding, and reasoning of the case, but you need to know more than that. You need to understand the case well enough that you are prepared to answer questions your professor will ask in class.

After you've read a case you should understand it at a sophisticated level. You should be able to tell me how the decision directly affects the two parties involved. You should have an opinion on whether the court applied the law correctly; whether the majority or the dissent have the more powerful argument; whether the case is consistent with cases previously discussed or consistent with other cases assigned for the day's reading. You should know which of the facts are most important and how the court's holding would change if you took one fact away. What is the slightest factual change that would lead to a different outcome? You should know why we are reading the case in this section of the chapter, rather than another. You should have an opinion on whether the court correctly applied precedent and, if not, why. Was precedent ignored because the judge believed justice required one party to prevail over another? Did public policy sway the court's decision? Only when you have done this for all of your assigned cases will you be "prepared for class."

E. Don't Forget the Book Notes

In preparing for class, read not only the cases assigned, but the notes that follow. For most casebooks, although not all, following a case will be a series of numbered paragraphs (called notes) that provide additional information about the case or the topic being studied, and usually ask questions of the reader.

Professors will often assign the notes as part of your reading. Even if the notes are not part of your assigned reading, you should read them because they provide guidance in analyzing the case and can assist you in figuring out how the case fits into the chapter. For some casebooks, the only way to understand a heavily edited case is to read the notes. Read the notes and think about the questions asked. If a note tells you to look something up, look it up.

F. Immediately Before Class

Arrive early to class. Unless your course schedule prevents it, you should arrive approximately fifteen minutes early to review your notes and prepare for class.

Professors usually start class by reviewing what was already covered. You must be prepared to answer questions related to the information you learned in the previous class. A professor's questions during this review time are the easiest questions to answer because they are *review* questions. The professor has already covered the topic. Right before class, go back and look at your notes from the day before. Familiarize yourself with the points covered so when asked a question you can respond.

Once you have reviewed the material from the previous class, move on to reviewing the cases that were assigned for that day's class. Remind yourself of the facts, issues, and holdings of the cases. Think about how the new cases fit in to what was already discussed. Anticipate what will be covered in the next lecture. Anticipate what questions will be asked.

During Class

Part of studying effectively depends on what you do in class. During class you must take selective notes, listen carefully to your classmates, and avoid being overly reliant on your laptop.

A. Listen Carefully

An obvious point: you must listen carefully. Sit up and pay attention. Sit in a place in class where it's easy for you to see the professor and stay alert. Make sure you've slept enough so you don't nod off or daydream. If you can't hear what the professor is saying, move closer to the front of the classroom.

B. Take Selective Notes

Law school is not like college. You must not write down everything said in class. You will feel pressure to. You may want to, but you should not. The best students take selective notes.

I will let you in on a little secret law professors have. Here it is: professors rarely say more than one or two important things in an hour class.

Most of what they say is useless. If you write down everything, you will be lost in piles of paper with disorganized, useless information. If you write down everything, life around exam time is going to be painful. If you take selective notes, your notes will be a great resource for studying.

Writing down everything said is easy. To be discriminating is difficult. By writing everything down, you distract yourself from the real point of class — thinking about the material. Write legibly. Write only key points. What is the rule? What is the policy? What is the key reasoning? What is the professor's opinion? That's what your notes should reflect.

Now, don't misunderstand me. You must take *some* notes. Notes are important. By writing notes and then working with those notes immediately after class, you retain and learn the material better. Notes are critical for later preparing for exams. By taking notes, you can keep track of items you do not understand, material you need to read, and important points your professor has emphasized. Put a star by the points the professor repeated numerous times so you can remember later that those points were critical. However, keep your notes succinct, short, and easy to understand. Figure that balance out and you will get much more out of law school.

More important than taking notes is what you do with them. Immediately after class, before you leave the classroom, look over your notes. It will take about ten minutes. Jot down the two or three key points from the lecture. Highlight important things. Make your notes more legible. Review. This is the time to ensure that you understood what the class was all about.

A final point on this. If your professor uses PowerPoint, please do not copy down everything from every slide. Sure, copying down everything may help you improve your typing speed. It will not help you be a lawyer. Lawyers do not transcribe. If you want to transcribe, become a court reporter.

C. Take Consistent and Organized Notes

Not only should your notes be selective, your notes should be consistent in style and format, and they should be organized. Consider including a heading for the first page of every day of notes (e.g., date, topic, etc.). Some students take notes in an outline format, others use mind-mapping software, and others use a note-taking software. Whatever you choose, be certain to be consistent. After a semester, you may have a hundred of pages of notes for a course. Organizing the notes as you write will make the notes more useful when you later review.

One important caveat: whatever format or style you choose, it should be simple and straightforward. If the format becomes too elaborate, note-taking will focus your efforts away from what the law professor is saying. You do not want to be distracted with mind-numbing details such as whether you should create a sub-heading or a sub-sub-heading, or whether that particular note should be in green, blue, or red.

D. Listen to Your Classmates

You may feel that most of class is spent with your classmates' amateur and unsophisticated attempts to analyze what the law is or should be. Some of your fellow students, bored by these exchanges, will be lured into playing solitaire or checking social media. Resist these temptations. Listen to what your classmates are saying.

Why? Because by listening to your classmates you learn how to discern between good and bad arguments. Class time is meant to enhance your analytical skills. On an exam you will include only strong arguments. The process of listening to your classmates will help you discern between strong and weak arguments and analysis.

By listening to your classmates, you will also better understand your professor's response to their answers. In doing so, you will start to develop an understanding of what the expectations are for the exam. Your professor will rarely tell you an answer. Rather, you will need to develop a sense of how your professor wants you to approach the law based on listening to the questions asked and the response to your classmate's answer.

Do not spend class time getting ready for the next case. You may think it's wise to use the time when your friend is answering a question to review for the next case in the chance you are next. This is another form of distraction. When a question is asked of one of your classmates, you should attempt to answer the question quietly yourself, and then evaluate how your answer compares to your classmate's. Be sure you understand the legal issues being discussed so you know if you have any questions that you need to ask.

Ultimately, if you don't stay focused on the discussion, when called on it will not matter whether you were surfing the internet or studying for the next case — you will not have heard the question and will be forced to ask,

"Can you repeat the question?" Which is really just another way of saying, "Sorry, Professor, I haven't been listening!"

After Class

How you approach studying after class is equally important as how you approach studying to prepare for class.

A. As Class Ends

After class review is as important, if not more important, than preparing before class. Spend ten minutes after each class reviewing what you covered in class, and writing down the key points your professor emphasized. Were your case briefs complete? How did this material relate to other material that you've covered in other classes? What new rules did you learn? Spending just a few minutes after class ensures that you understand the material and gives you an opportunity to identify any lingering questions you may have on a topic while the topic is fresh in your mind. If something is unclear, now is the time to discuss it with your study group or with the professor.

B. Use Your Professor Effectively

One of the most valuable and under-used resources in law school are your professors. Many students go to the bookstore and load up on hornbooks, commercial outlines, case summaries, various supplements, review books, and exam prep materials. Yet they fail to avail themselves of the number one learning support opportunity — talking one on one with a professor.

Visiting your professors in office hours is essential. Not only will you get your questions answered, but you will begin to establish a relationship. Developing a professional, personal relationship with your professor can be one of the more rewarding aspects of law school and a powerful strategy for future success. A majority of your professors will be experts in their field. They may have practiced and will be able to give you advice about your career. They will also be in the position to write you the strongest letters of recommendation and serve as references and contacts for future employment opportunities. Don't walk into a professor's office and ask the professor for a letter of recommendation after introducing yourself for the first time. Professors only write letters for those they know.

If a professional relationship is not a sufficient motivation to visit your professor, then go to office hours to help improve your preparation for the final exam. Who better to ask about what is expected on the exam than the one writing the exam? You will discover a lot about exam expectations and style just by talking with your professor during office hours. Many professors will grade a practice exam for you and will be happy to discuss the results of the exam in office hours. These discussions can lead to invaluable insight into the depth of analysis and organization they expect of their students.

Regardless of this advice, many of you will not take advantage of the opportunity to visit your professors during office hours. Some of you will feel you have no questions, so you will assume you do not need to see the professor. Others, who are struggling, may be too embarrassed to ask a question. Still others will assume the professors are too busy to be bothered with student questions.

Ignore these feelings as they surface throughout the semester. If you don't have a question, identify a legal issue that came up in class that you would like to discuss further. If you are embarrassed or worried about intruding — get over it! Keep in mind that professors genuinely enjoy helping students. It is the part of the job that we love. Professors sit through committee meetings, perform inane administrative tasks, grade endless amounts of exams, all so we can do what we love, teaching! Coming to a professor for help may turn out to be the highlight of their day because they actually were able to teach.

C. Limits on Using Your Professor

Although building a relationship with your professors is important, a line exists between appropriate and inappropriate contact with your professor. Unless you are struggling and need special assistance, a visit once or twice a month is sufficient. If your professor offers large group office hours where all students are invited to come and ask questions, don't miss them. Even if you do not have any questions, you will likely learn something from one the questions your classmates ask. These sessions do not count towards your monthly visits.

A note on email — in today's society, sometimes it seems easier to simply shoot off an email rather than go into office hours. This is appropriate when your question is discrete and requires a short response. Any question that involves a complex discussion of legal issues should be addressed during office hours.

D. Using Study Groups Effectively

For those of you who base your expectations of law school on what you have seen in movies like *Legally Blonde*, study groups may seem like the end-all, be-all of the law school experience. However, relying on study groups, if they become your primary method of studying, can be detrimental to your law school career. Study groups should play a useful, but probably a limited, role in your study regime.

Study groups are helpful because they allow you to talk out ideas which can be helpful in developing your analytical skills. Reviewing class materials with others will point out any holes in your outlines and allow you to find out if you missed a concept or definition that is important to know. Study groups provide a forum for you to quiz each other, allow you to share studying techniques, and present you with different perspectives or approaches to the law that you had not thought of before.

There are different approaches to study groups. A study group may meet on a weekly basis to go over what was covered in class that week. A study group might get together only at the end of the semester to prepare for finals. Other groups meet each morning as a way to prepare for class. No matter what approach a study group takes, it should not be the primary source of studying. To be effective, all the students in group must be committed to the group and contribute.

Choose your study group partners carefully. For you to get the most out of your study group, you need study partners who are also willing to do the work before they get to the group. You need people who are focused on studying, not socializing. Keeping your study group to a small number is often wise — perhaps three or four students. Study groups with too many students become inefficient. For the group to be effective, each member of the group must have time to participate and talk. A good use of a study group is to take practice exams. The group can take an exam under timed conditions and then exchange answers so that other members of the group can critique them.

A few "don'ts" with study groups. Do not join a study group to socialize. Do not join a study group to lessen the work load. Do not divide courses and assign each person an outline to do. This is one of the dangers of study groups and a mistake. The point of creating outlines is the learning process. Outlining allows you to organize your notes and thoughts in a way that the material makes logical sense. You are preparing for exams as you are outlining. By relying on someone else's outline you run the risk of missing important concepts: trying to study from someone else's outline is an exercise in futility.

A study group should be used to review concepts discussed in class and as a sounding board for ideas. If you join a study group in which the members want to divide the work, this is an indicator that you have a group of people who are looking for the easy road. Find a new group. If your study group routinely meets in a bar, where more drinking is done than studying, this is also an indicator that it is time to find a new group.

E. As the Semester Ends

As the semester nears the end, your studying should focus less on preparing for class, and more on getting ready to take final exams. Be sure to study each subject separately. Don't fall into the trap of studying too extensively for one course and too little for others.

In the last four-to-five weeks of the semester, spend most of your time learning actively. Passive learning involves reading and reviewing outlines. Active learning includes finishing your outlining, writing up flashcards, and taking practice exams. You want to use the materials you are studying.

You'll be busy. As the semester ends, you can expect to be working 10–12 hours a day (including class time). If you put in the work, you will be happier with the results.

Checklist Reminders

The Basics

- ❑ *Create a study schedule (three hours of study for each hour of class)*
- ❑ *Study in a quiet, distraction-free place*
- ❑ *Read all assigned cases carefully (don't forget the notes!)*
- ❑ *Immediately before class review notes, cases, and briefs*
- ❑ *Immediately after class review class notes (what were the key points?)*

❑ *Study actively (write and create, and take practice exams, don't just review)*

❑ *Study a lot! Law school is like a full-time job*

During Class

❑ *Engage and listen carefully*

❑ *Take selective notes*

❑ *No surfing the internet during class*

❑ *Take consistent, organized notes in a straightforward format*

❑ *Pay attention to classmates when they are asked questions (what is the professor focusing on?)*

Notes on Study Groups

❑ *Choose group carefully*

❑ *Keep small (perhaps three or four students)*

❑ *Agree on group expectations and goals*

❑ *Stay focused during study group meetings (not the time to socialize!)*

❑ *Don't divide up outlines*

❑ *Don't meet in pubs and bars (darn! is there no fun in law school...)*

6

FINAL EXAMS

Musings of a cranky professor....

Time to grade exams. The worst part of my job. If only I could put it off for one more day, but I have to start. I open the first exam. It starts by restating every fact from the exam question, as if I don't know what the facts are. As if I did not write them. I'm not up for this. I put it down and open a second exam.

Exam two. The student writing this exam rambles on and on about every rule under the sun. The exam continues for pages and pages. No organization. No arguments about how the rules apply to the facts. Only a few facts are even mentioned. My head hurts. I can't understand what this student is saying. I put it aside and try another exam.

Exam three. Fingers crossed. Please be good...

What is this? What is happening? My exam question was straightforward. A clear call of the question, centered at the bottom of the page: "Should the court grant the motion to dismiss?" And then next to it, in bold: "The court has jurisdiction. Do not discuss any jurisdictional issues." So how does this student's exam begin? "The first issue is whether the court has jurisdiction." I'm stunned. Completely baffled. It then proceeds for two full pages to set out elaborate jurisdictional rules, only to conclude: "But as the exam says, the court has jurisdiction, so no further analysis is needed." This is painful.

I let out a tiny sigh. It's going to be a long night. Tomorrow in class I'll tell my students how they should prepare for and write an essay exam....

Before the Exam

To do well in law school you must do well on your final exams. Law school is different from many graduate programs. Usually for first-year courses, students will take one exam at the end of the semester worth 100% of the grade. It doesn't matter how brilliant you were in class, or whether you understood the subtleties of the law, or whether you are beloved by your professor. If you don't do well on the final exam, you've got nothing.

Most first-year essay exams follow a standard format: they set out a complex fact pattern, pose a hypothetical legal problem, and then ask you to resolve that problem. To do well, you must: (1) spot the relevant legal issues; (2) identify the legal rules applicable to those issues; (3) identify the key facts upon which each issue turns; and (4) draw a conclusion in a logical, analytical way. Rarely will an exam have one "right" answer. Your conclusion is much less important than your analysis and how you reach the conclusion.

Law school exams are also not like college exams. In your undergraduate classes, you could parrot back the information you read and do fine. You might even do well. Not so in law school. For law school exams, you must apply the legal principles you have learned to a new factual context. Merely spitting back rules that you have memorized is worth little. Writing everything you know about the course will not suffice. You have to do more. You must write a clear, concise, and thoughtful answer to the legal question posed.

This all too abstract? Okay. Here are some specific guidelines for getting prepared for your final exams.

A. Know Your Professor

You are not just writing an exam; you are writing an exam for a specific professor. This is important. Each professor has their own quirks and requirements. To do well, you must have a sense of how your professor will test you and how the professor will grade the exam. Will the exam be open book? Closed book? Take-home? Does the professor use essay questions, multiple choice, something else? What is the professor looking for in an answer?

The best way to figure out how a professor will test is to look at the professor's prior exams. Many schools require that professors either post exams online or hold them on reserve in the school's library. You should look at a course's past exams early on in the semester. Within the first few weeks of the course, you want a sense of how the professor will evaluate you so that you may tailor your studying and preparation.

B. Keep Your Outline Updated

Daily preparation matters. You will not do well in law school if you cram all your studying into the final weeks of the term. Keeping your course outline up to date is critical. Each week, you should review the material you've learned from the prior week and place it in your outline. Keeping your outline updated is also a good way of seeing how different cases covered in class fit into the larger topics you are studying. Your outline is your primary study tool for the final exam — don't forget it.

C. Schedule Practice Exams

Do not wait until the end of the semester or until you have completed your outline to start taking practice exams. One of the biggest mistakes a student can make is to wait to take practice exams until after they have finished all their studying, outlines, and briefs. You want to start taking practice exams early in the semester.

Practicing is the best way to improve and to learn the law, so reserve specific time to practice. At the start of the semester, set up a schedule to ensure that you will have time set aside to take sufficient practice exams. Starting in the fourth week of the semester, you should take as many as two timed, practice essay exams each week. Generally this will mean that you will take a practice exam in a particular subject once every two weeks.

Ideally, you should take six or more practice one-hour essay exams for each course that you are enrolled in. Since law school exams are generally different from other sorts of tests that students have previously encountered, students who write out practice exams are less likely to be shocked when they face their first real exam. If any of your professors use multiple-choice tests, you should also answer hundreds of practice multiple-choice questions before the actual exam.

Usually, your professor will make past exams available. If your professor does, take advantage of it. Your own professor's exams are the best place to turn to first. If your professor, however, does not have past exams, you can easily find samples. There's plenty of sample first-year exams on the internet, and most libraries will carry commercial exam preparation guides. Ideally, however, you want to practice exams that are similar to your professor's style and format.

D. Approach Practice Exams Effectively

Make sure you take some of the practice exams under timed conditions. You can always revisit the exam afterwards to study the legal issues the exam raises more thoroughly, but the benefit is that you get to experience the practice exam under similar conditions as your final exam. If your final exam will be a one-hour essay exam, you should limit your response time on your practice exam to one hour. If your final exam will be closed book (i.e., no notes), your practice exam should also be closed book. If your final exam will be open book, your practice exam should be open book. By taking timed practice exams, you will hone your test-taking skills. This includes honing your ability to: (1) allocate your time, (2) identify areas of law that you don't understand; (3) spot issues; and (4) work under pressure. Most exams are time-pressured. So taking an exam under timed conditions is critical to doing well. Don't worry if early in the semester you find it difficult to answer the question. You will improve with each practice exam you take.

E. Learn How Your Professor Grades

Not only do you want to know what each professor's exams look like, you want to know how the professors grade. Some professors spend hours closely scrutinizing exams; others read them very quickly. Some use a point system that awards you credit for the mere mention of an argument, while others focus more on how skillfully you make the argument. Some take points off for incorrect answers, others only award points for correct answers. Some award points for creative, push-the-boundary type arguments, while some professors award no points for them. Some professors care about how well you write, while others are not concerned about writing style, grammar, or punctuation at all. Find out what your professor cares about, and make sure you meet those expectations. If your professors offer to review your written work and provide feedback, take them up on their offers.

F. Go to Review Sessions

For many courses, professors will hold exam workshops or review sessions. Sometimes professors teach these sessions, other times they are taught by teaching assistants. If your professor holds an exam workshop, attendance is not optional (no matter what the professor says). Often professors will consciously, or subconsciously, give exam tips during the review sessions. Review sessions are a good way to get insight into what your particular professor is looking for in an answer. The same is true if professors use teaching assistants. Meeting with teaching assistants is often a means to get information about the professor, how the professor grades, and what is most likely to be tested on the exam.

A related point. Most schools these days have very sophisticated academic support programs or offices. Experts on learning and law school teach and direct these programs. Often schools will have student mentors, writing centers, exam workshops, and a variety of other support programs. Look for these resources and use them. Ignoring these resources will put you at a disadvantage to those classmates who are taking advantage of them.

G. Know the Legal Rules Cold

Knowing the law (i.e., the legal rules) that you have studied during the semester is a prerequisite to doing well. Knowing the law won't guarantee you a good grade, but not knowing the law will guarantee a poor grade, and possibly a failing one.

You have to know the rules down cold. A final exam is time-pressured. You will not have time to think through or look up the relevant law (even if it's an open-book, open-notes exam). Instead, you have to be comfortable enough with the law that once you spot an issue, you can quickly set out the legal standard, test, or factors that determine how the legal issue should be resolved.

This doesn't mean that you should mindlessly memorize legal rules. Simple memorization is the wrong emphasis. Instead, you will know the rules by heart because you have seen them in the cases you read, included them in your case briefs, reviewed them before class, discussed them in class, studied them after class and in study groups, included them in your outline, and used them when writing practice exams.

H. No All-Nighters and Manage Stress

Law school exams require you to think and be on your game. If you stay up all night studying in the days leading up to an exam, you will be tired. If you're tired, you won't be able to focus, and if you are not able to give the exam the focus you need, you will do poorly. More importantly, you'll be wiped out for the next exam. Because many students take three to five exams over an approximate two-week exam period, pulling all-nighters is a recipe for disaster. You must get a good night's sleep before the exam.

During the exam period, you should eat well, and get enough sleep and exercise. This is critical. Managing stress and staying healthy is as important to doing well as how you study. Establishing these routines now will also help you manage stress and keep a work-life balance once you begin to practice law.

Starting the Exam

So what you should you do on the day of the exam and at the very start of the exam?

A. Arrive Early

You have enough things to worry about, don't add additional stress by arriving late to the exam. Arrive 20–30 minutes early (some schools require that you arrive even earlier). Be sure that you know where your exam will be given, or give yourself plenty of time to find the exam room. Arriving early will also allow you to select a good place to sit during the exam. Select a spot to take the test that enables you to have enough space to work. Do not go to an exam on an empty stomach. Be sure to eat before going to an exam (drinking five cups of coffee and pounding cans of red bull is not eating).

B. Arrive Prepared

An obvious point: Be sure you arrive prepared, with sufficient pens, pencils, and highlighters, or whatever else you plan to use on the exam. Ensure that your laptop is working properly and that any exam-taking software the school requires is working well.

You also should dress comfortably, and be ready for different room conditions (think layers, so that you can adapt to excessive air-conditioners, broken heaters, and the like). Many schools will permit you to bring a silent, non-digital (analog) timer to the exam, as well as calculators, ear-plugs, and even snacks. Figure out beforehand what your school permits, and come prepared.

Right before the exam is not the time to start cramming. Relax. You've studied hard. You will do fine. Nothing in the last few minutes before the exam will change how you will do, but it could unnecessarily add to the stress. Try to avoid last-minute panic conversations with your classmates about course topics in the few minutes leading up to the exam.

C. Read the Instructions

The first thing you should do is read the instructions carefully, and then follow them. If the exam says, "write a memo" — you will write a memo. If the exam says, assume a certain fact — you will assume that fact. If an exam says, do not address an issue — you will not address that issue. If the exam tells you to play a role (e.g., to write a bench memo as a judge's clerk, or serve as the attorney for the defendant), then be sure to play that role. It doesn't matter what the instructions say, you will follow them.

Reading the instructions carefully sounds like common sense, but every year students forget. Some of the most unfortunate exam mistakes (i.e., not answering the question asked, running out of time, or focusing on incorrect issues) can be traced to the student's failure to carefully read the exam instructions.

D. Allocate Your Time

After carefully reading the instructions, you should flip through the exam and allocate the time you intend to spend on each section of the exam. You should also allocate how much time you can spend on each question within an exam section.

This is important. If the exam tells you how much time to spend on each question, then do exactly what the exam tells you. If the exam does not specify, then allocate your time based on the relative worth of the exam question. If you have a two-hour exam, with two essay questions, spend one hour on each essay. If it's a two-hour exam, and one essay is worth 60% and the other 40%, spend 72 minutes on the first question, and 48 minutes on the second (I know, crazy math, but you'll figure it out). Once you have allocated your time, follow it strictly. If you allocate an hour to the first essay and the hour is up — you must move on.

Do not fall into the trap of spending all your time on one question. Many students when starting law school make this mistake. You must answer every question asked in the exam to do well. An "A" grade on the first essay, and an "F" grade on the second essay — it still a C grade. An amazing answer on the first question will never make up for the last question you did not answer. Allocate your time and stick with it. Once your time is up for one part of the exam, stop and move on.

E. Read the Call of the Question

For most essay exams, the professor will have a "call of the question" — sometimes referred to as an interrogatory — at the end of a fact pattern. The "call" will tell you what the professor wants you to do. After you have allocated your time, you should turn to the first essay question and read the call of that essay question carefully. Read the call of the question before you read the fact pattern. This way when you read the fact pattern you will more easily be able to spot the significance of certain facts.

This related point seems too basic, but it is one of the most common mistakes students make: answer the question that your professors asks. I do not want an essay on everything we discussed in the course. If I ask you: "Should the court dismiss for reason X," your answer must focus on reason X. Do not discuss anything else. The question was specific, and your answer must be specific too. Exam answers that do not answer the question asked will not be passing exam answers. Discussing topics that are not relevant to the question asked is wasting time. You will not earn points for those discussions.

F. Read the Facts (and Again)

After you have read the call of the question, read the fact pattern. You should read it once. Then you should read it again. And perhaps again. Understanding the facts may be the most important part of the exam. In a one-hour exam question, the first five to ten minutes should be spent just reading the exam and ensuring that you understand what is being asked. Consider highlighting, circling, or underlining key points or facts in the exam. If a fact is included in the question, you should likely discuss or use it in your answer. A common mistake by law students is to not talk enough about the facts in their exam answers. Law professors want students to talk about the law in a particular factual context. So spending time to carefully read and understand the question's fact pattern is time well spent.

G. Outline Your Answer

You have read the instructions, allocated your time, read the call of the question and the facts carefully — now you should outline your answer. You must spend time thinking through your answer before you start writing. Doing so will help you spot the key issues and organize your answer. Students who organize their answer almost always do better on exams. A short outline ensures that: (1) you don't forget to discuss key points you intend to discuss; and (2) that you stay organized.

You will feel pressure to start writing immediately. Don't. Even if the person next to you starts madly tapping away at the keyboard, you will ensure that you've spent a few minutes thinking through your answer and how to organize it. As a rule of thumb, in a one-hour essay exam, your total time for reading the call, reading the facts, and outlining should take approximately 15–20 minutes, depending on how detailed your outline is. You must leave enough time (at least 40–45 minutes) to write your answer.

Students who do not outline spend pages discussing the issues in a me-andering way, often describing obscure and unlikely arguments. Students who have spent time outlining know that four or five issues must be covered and the time they have to cover each issue. That student is far more likely to provide an analysis that adheres to the relevant legal and factual issues, and will do well. An exam answer that is a stream of consciousness will not do well. Exams are not about getting down as much on paper as possible. You must provide an organized and logical response to the question asked.

How do you outline an exam answer? Start by jotting down the main issues that the essay question raises in the order you will address them: battery, assault, intentional infliction of emotional distress, etc. Then break down each main issue into its elements. Start by including one sub-section for each element. For example, under your heading for assault, you might list conduct by defendant, intent to cause plaintiff apprehension of harm, and plaintiff's apprehension of harm.

Next, look at the facts your professor provided in the exam answer. Jot down the most relevant facts within each element. Note, some facts often fit into more than one issue/element. In this case, include the fact in all relevant issues/elements. As you jot down the facts, you may suddenly think of additional relevant issues. Excellent. Add those to your outline as well.

When you are finished, you will visibly see which legal issues are the most important issues to discuss on the exam. The issues with the most relevant "facts" are the critical issues worth most of the points. Your exam answer should address all of the relevant legal issues in your outline, but you should pay special attention to the topics that are directly related to the most facts. This will help you time-manage as well. You should spend most of your time on the most relevant issues.

Writing the Exam

How should you write a law school exam? Professors have differing advice. But here are a few tips that most commonly agree on.

A. Use IRAC

When writing an exam, organize your answer using "IRAC." IRAC is acronym that stands for Issue, Rule, Analysis, and Conclusion. IRAC is a useful tool for organizing an answer to a law school essay exam and an effective method of legal analysis.

The basic IRAC structure is fairly straightforward: for each legal issue raised, you must set out the legal rules before you apply those rules to the facts provided in the exam question. Here are the steps:

1. Issue: For each question asked in an exam, identify the relevant legal issues and create a heading for each issue.
2. Rule: Within each heading, state the legal rules related to that legal issue.
3. Application: After stating all rules relevant to the issue, apply those rules to the exam's facts provided by your professor.
4. Conclusion: Finally, state your conclusion.

Let's walk through each of these steps in more detail.

B. "I": The Issue

Issue spotting is the first essential aspect of writing a high scoring law school exam. Each exam will include a fact pattern which you will need to analyze to determine the legal issues relevant to the call of the question. Professors spend considerable time designing fact patterns for the final exams. The facts in the patterns will touch on many different aspects of the course materials. If you cannot spot the important legal issues to be analyzed in a particular fact pattern, you will not be successful on your exams.

In some cases, there may be only one issue in the fact pattern that you must spot and analyze. On the majority of exams, however, the facts will be crafted carefully to ensure that there are several issues for students to "spot" and analyze in their answer. Each fact pattern will likely include issues which are obvious — the ones your professor expects all or most students to spot, but there will also be more subtle or hidden issues which are harder to spot. The professor designs these to discover which students have a thorough understanding of the course material, as well as top analytical skills, to separate the "A" students from the "C" students. As such, the importance of issue spotting cannot be exaggerated. Each legal issue embedded in the fact pattern will be worth points on the exam based on your analysis of that issue. If you fail to spot an issue in the fact pattern, you will lose all points related to that issue.

The only way to become proficient in the skill of issue spotting is to practice. Get in those reps! The more practice exams you take, the more fact patterns you read, the better you will become at picking out the key words and key facts that trigger an issue which needs to be analyzed in your exam answer. As you take practice exams throughout the semester, you will begin to see patterns in the way the facts are organized or the scenarios used by professors to test a particular legal rule. It will allow you to anticipate how your professor will test a particular rule on the final exam.

There is no greater technique for improving your issue spotting skills than to take a large number of practice exams. However, there are a few other strategies that can also be helpful both before and during the exam. To increase your chances of spotting all the issues on the exam, use your study outline to create a checklist of issues prior to the exam. Keeping the checklist in your head as you read each fact pattern on the exam will help ensure you do not miss any important issues. During the exam, analyze each fact with your issue checklist in mind. Determine how each fact might be relevant to one of the legal issues on your checklist. Professors sometimes include irrelevant facts, as red herrings, but these will be few. The majority of facts in the fact pattern have been specifically included to be relevant to one or more issues the professor expects you to analyze, so if you find that you have not used most of the facts in your answer, go back and look again at each fact to be sure you have not missed a crucial issue. Finally, as stated above, it is worth taking the time to outline your answer prior to writing, as it decreases the likelihood that you will miss an issue in your haste to complete the answer in the time allotted.

When it comes to writing your answer, you also want to visually organize your answer around the issues. One tip to keep in mind is that professors hate grading. Grading cuts into time that could be spent writing, researching, speaking at conferences, preparing for class, spending time with family, or taking a vacation. Professors don't have time, and won't make time, to suss out every point that you made or could have made on your exam. In short, you must make it simple for your professor to follow your analysis.

This means you must use headings and subheadings to break up the different issues in the exam. Headings make your exam answer easier to read and will reveal your logical organization. Headings should be organized around the issues you have spotted in your analysis of the exam question.

Assume your exam states that Defendant chased Plaintiff down the street with a baseball bat, yelling "I am going to kill you." Plaintiff ran into Company's store, slipped and fell, and was severely injured. The exam asks you to analyze Plaintiff's claims against Defendant AND Plaintiff's claims against the Company. Thus, you have two calls of the question and would start with two headings: "Plaintiff's Claim against Defendant" and "Plaintiff's Claims against Company." Bold each heading that relates to a call of the question.

Each call of the question should then be broken down by legal issues, in this case claims that Plaintiff could bring against either Defendant or Company. For each legal issues, have one heading indicating the name of the issue. Start with the first call of the question: Plaintiff's claims against the Defendant. Within that bolded topic, list all relevant legal issues. You might have a heading for battery, assault, intentional infliction of emotional distress, etc.

1. **Plaintiff's Claims against Defendant**
   Battery
   Assault
   Intentional Infliction of Emotional Distress

Next step: sub-headings. You should have one subheading for each specific legal element within the main issue. Let's break down "assault" as an example. Assume for the purposes of our example that "assault" has three elements: (i) voluntary act by the defendant; (ii) intent to create apprehension of harmful conduct; and (iii) causation of apprehension of imminent harmful contact. Each of these elements is its own legal element and deserves its own heading. So your headings start to look more like this:

1. Plaintiff's Claims against Defendant
<u>Battery</u>
<u>Assault</u>
  <u>1. Voluntary Act by the Defendant</u>
  <u>2. Intent to Create Apprehension of Harmful Contact</u>
  <u>3. Caused Apprehension of Harmful Contact</u>
<u>Intentional Infliction of Emotional Distress</u>

Quick note on the visual organization of your answer: bold the calls of the question, but underline all headings related to a legal issue. Do not bold and underline. Do not italicize. Just underline. Keep it simple and it will be easier for your professor to read. The more you bold, italicize, use all CAPS, etc., the harder the paper is to read. In fact, the varying fonts and typeface can make your professor nauseous. Keep it simple. Just list the legal topic within each call of the question and underline it. Indent and underline sub-headings.

Try to refrain from using sub-sub-headings. Headings are necessary, but too many headings makes the essay hard to follow. Use sub-sub headings only when absolutely necessary. Never use sub-sub-sub headings. Note, these are general guidelines. Every exam is different and you will need to adopt your headings to fit the specifics of your exam and your professor's preferences.

Now that you have the background necessary to know how to set up your legal issues, let's talk about what to draft within each issue. For each legal issue identified, you will typically draft one complete IRAC. Thus, the issue "voluntary act by the defendant" would be followed by its own Rule, Application, and Conclusion. "Intent to create apprehension of harmful contact" and "Caused of apprehension of harmful conduct" would also each be followed by their own IRACs. Once you break down the torts of Battery and Intentional Infliction of Emotional Distress into their elements, you would draft one IRAC for each of those sub-elements as well. For the "I" component of the IRAC, most professors will be satisfied with the heading alone as a way to identify the Issue. Some professors, however, will want you to draft the legal issue as a complete sentence following the heading. For example, below the heading on voluntary act, you would state: "The issue is whether the defendant made a voluntary act." Follow the directions of your professor. The critical task in drafting the "I" part of the IRAC is to identify the legal issues and set up those legal issues in an organized manner. Once you have set forth the issues, remember to do an independent IRAC for each legal issue/element.

C. "R": The Rule

When writing an exam, you must set out the legal rules clearly, succinctly, and precisely. Some study guides recommend you skip the rules and incorporate them in your answer. Don't listen to them. Unless your professor tells you otherwise, this is terrible advice. You must set out the rules for each issue/sub-issue before you apply the rules to the facts. Precision in law matters. It is not okay to get the rule "kind of right." "Kind of right" is equal to wrong. Professors generally do not require specific case names, but you should know the elements of each of the relevant legal issues.

When you write the rules, try to frame the general rule in terms of elements. Do not provide the history of the legal rule. Simply state the elements of the rule and any relevant policy (if applicable). One trick to drafting your rule is to include the word "if," "when," or "must" in your sentence. A plaintiff can win *if* (i), (ii), and (iii) are met. An assault occurs *when* (i), (ii), and (iii). To prevail on assault, plaintiff *must* show (i), (ii), and (iii). Here is a portion of an exam answer for Assault with the rules included:

Assault

Overview of
General Rule

To prevail on assault, plaintiff must show defendant (i) voluntarily acted; (ii) intended to create apprehension of imminent harmful or offensive conduct; and (iii) caused reasonable apprehension of imminent harmful or offensive conduct.

1. Voluntary Act by the Defendant

Defendant must have taken a voluntary action. The defendant does not need to make contact with the plaintiff. However, words alone are sufficient to create an assault. The defendant must have some conduct or other circumstances in addition to words. The defendant's actions must be voluntarily.

Rule for
1st Element

2. Intent to Create Apprehension of Harmful Contact

To satisfy intent, the defendant must desire the plaintiff to experience apprehension of harmful or offensive conduct or know with substantial likelihood such apprehension would occur. Defendant's own words can negate the element of intent.

Rule for
2nd Element

3. Caused Apprehension of Harmful Contact

In order to qualify as an assault, the defendant must cause plaintiff to experience reasonable apprehension of harmful or offensive conduct. Fear is not equivalent to apprehension. Reasonable apprehension occurs so long as (i) the plaintiff believes harmful or offensive conduct is imminent; and (ii) the plaintiff's belief is justified under the circumstances. Threats of future harm are insufficient.

Rule for
3rd Element

Notice this exam started by stating the overarching elements in an introduction paragraph and then stated the specific rule for each element within the heading for that element.

Final tip: avoid a rule dump. Your exam answer is not the forum to recite all rules on your outline in the hope you will get credit for knowing the rules. Your professor is evaluating whether you can identify the relevant legal rules that are applicable to the facts provided in the fact pattern and the issues identified. Rule dumps do not earn passing exam scores.

D. "A": The Application

The application part of IRAC is where you will demonstrate your analysis of the law. Your analysis involves applying the facts provided in the exam problem to the rules you have set forth in the Rule portion of your exam. When drafting the application section of your answer, it is essential that you (i) use the specific facts from the exam question, (ii) use the exact terminology of the rules you set forth in your exam answer, (iii) use the word "because" to link the rules to your facts; and (iv) address all appropriate counter-arguments.

Let's start with the facts set forth in your exam question. You must use them. All of them. At least almost all of them. When drafting the application section, facts are critical. Legal analysis boils down to discussing the law in the context of particular facts. Lawyers get paid to identify relevant facts from irrelevant facts and then apply the law to the facts. For this reason, an answer that merely recites canned rules or cases is deficient. Exams that merely state conclusions will also earn a low grade. To earn a top grade, you must apply the legal rules to the facts provided. You must demonstrate you understand the nuances of the facts and the relevance of the details. Do not simply restate or summarize the facts. You must link them to the law and show that you understand why certain facts are significant and why the facts of the particular problem lead you to a particular conclusion. Professors spend considerable time incorporating key facts in an exam question. You must be certain to incorporate them and discuss them in your answer. By the time your exam answer is finished, you should have used almost every fact from the exam. Finally, remember to be specific when referencing the facts. Do not generalize facts by stating the defendant attacked the plaintiff. Include the details: The defendant chased the plaintiff down the street while holding a baseball bat and swinging it in the air violently.

Next, the terminology or wording used in your application matters. When you apply the rules to the facts, it is important to use the exact wording of the rules you set forth in the rule section of the exam answer and link that exact wording directly to the specific facts from the exam question. If your exam includes a rule that defendant's behavior must include "conduct in addition to words," your application should use the exact words "conduct in addition to words" For example, your argument might state: The defendant used conduct in addition to words because the defendant swung the baseball bat at the plaintiff. Do not change the terminology to state: The defendant's behavior included actions because the defendant swung the baseball bat at the plaintiff. Your reader will stop because the reader never heard the word "actions" as part of the rule. It will cause confusion and your reader will have to take the time to figure out that when you say "actions," you mean "conduct." Using the exact terminology from the Rule portion of the exam answer helps your reader easily see the connection between the rule and your argument.

Third tip for drafting the Application: use the word "because." To receive a high score on analysis, you cannot merely state an element has been met, you must explain how that element has been met. You must show how you reached your conclusions. You must show your work! To do this, use the word *because* liberally. Let's take a look at an example application for each of our three elements, using the word "because."

1. Voluntary Act by the Defendant

The defendant engaged in conduct other than mere words <u>because</u> the defendant was swinging the baseball bat at plaintiff as he chased the plaintiff down the street.

Application for 1st Element

2. Intent to Create Apprehension of Harmful Contact

The defendant intended to create apprehension of harmful or offensive conduct <u>because</u> the defendant was yelling at plaintiff "I am going to kill you" and most individuals know the fear of death would cause apprehension in another.

Application for 2nd Element

3. Caused Apprehension of Harmful Contact

The defendant's actions caused reasonable apprehension of harmful conduct <u>because</u> the plaintiff believed harm was imminent and the plaintiff's belief was justified. First, it was reasonable to believe the harm was imminent <u>because</u> the defendant waived the bat and chased after the plaintiff, indicating he would hit the plaintiff at the moment he caught up to the plaintiff. The defendant was not threatening to hurt plaintiff at some point in the future. Second, the plaintiff's belief of imminent harm was justified <u>because</u> bats are known to cause harm if contact is made between a bat and a person and the defendant could have caught up to the plaintiff and used it at any moment.

Application for 3rd Element

Notice the pattern? Each element is applied using the exact language from the legal rule followed by a "because" that incorporates the facts from the exam question. These applications for each element will be placed immediately following the rule for each element. Thus, each of these three applications would be placed under different headings. The application for voluntary act would be placed after the rule under the "voluntary act" heading. The application for intent would be placed after the rule under the "intent" heading. The application for causation would be placed after the rule under the "causation" heading. Here is an example of a complete IRAC for the causation element:

Caused Apprehension of Harmful Contact

Issue   In order to qualify as an assault, the defendant must cause plaintiff to experience reasonable apprehension of harmful or offensive conduct. Fear is not equivalent to apprehension. Reasonable apprehension occurs so long as (i) the plaintiff believes harmful or offensive conduct is imminent, and (ii) the plaintiff's belief is justified under the circumstances. Threats of future harm are insufficient.

Rule

Application   The defendant's actions caused reasonable apprehension of harmful conduct <u>because</u> the plaintiff believed harm was imminent and the plaintiff's belief was justified. First it was reasonable to believe harm was imminent because the defendant waived the bat and chased after the plaintiff, indicating he would hit the plaintiff at the moment he caught up to the plaintiff. The defendant was not threatening to hurt plaintiff at some point in the future. Second, the plaintiff's belief of imminent harm was justified under the circumstances <u>because</u> bats are known to cause harm if contact is made between a bat and a person and the defendant could have caught up to the plaintiff and used it any moment.

Conclusion   Therefore, the element of causation of apprehension is satisfied.

Final suggestion for your application section: argue both sides. For most law school exams you will have to analyze a number of different legal issues. Many (but not all) of these issues will be a "close call." A "close call" means the plaintiff and defendant both have strong arguments under the law: strong enough that making the argument would not draw laughter from a judge. If the facts create strong arguments for both the defendant and the plaintiff, you must provide both arguments and explain why you think one side of the argument will prevail over the other.

Let's take the hypothetical from above but assume the exam states that Defendant and Plaintiff were best friends and that prior to defendant chasing plaintiff down the street, Plaintiff and Defendant were joking about a time they saw a woman chase a man down the street with a bat. Based on these additional facts, can you see an argument for Defendant that his actions did not create an assault? Perhaps Defendant has a strong argument that he did not intend to create apprehension in the Plaintiff. Defendant could argue that he did not desire the Plaintiff to have apprehension or know with substantial certainty it would occur because Defendant thought the chase was merely a joke between friends. Reasonable people would not think a joke would cause apprehension in another. Perhaps Defendant also has a strong argument with respect to whether Defendant actually caused apprehension of imminent harm. Defendant could argue that Plaintiff did not actually experience apprehension because the two were best friends and Plaintiff would know Defendant would not actually hit Plaintiff with the bat. These are strong arguments for Defendant. Strong enough that they need to be addressed in your arguments.

There are various ways to organize the counter-arguments. Some of you will be naturally inclined to start the application of the law with the stronger arguments (i.e., the arguments for the party you think will prevail). This is an effective approach, but keep in mind if you start the application with the stronger arguments, you will need to follow the arguments with both counter-arguments and a rebuttal to the counter-arguments. An alternative approach to organizing counter-arguments, which can save you time, is to begin your application with the weaker arguments, followed by the stronger arguments. This alternative approach helps save time on the exam because you will not need a separate section for rebuttal. Under the "weaker argument first" approach, your response to the counter-arguments is simply included as part of the prevailing arguments that follow.

Regardless of which approach you choose, be sure to use clear transition sentences as you transition between arguments. If you start with the stronger arguments, transition to the weaker arguments by stating, "On the other hand, the opposing side can argue...." If you start with the weaker arguments, transition to the stronger arguments by stating, "These arguments are likely to fail." Your writing must let your reader know you are transitioning from one argument to the other.

You will not argue both sides for every element or even for every main topic. Whether a counter-argument should be included depends on the facts of the case. Include a counter-argument anytime the facts indicate there are two opposing strong arguments.

E. "C": The Conclusion

Arguing both sides does not mean that you can avoid answering the question asked. You must provide a conclusion, and tell the professor which arguments are strong and which are weak. Too often students write an "on-the-one-hand-on-the-other-hand" examination without reaching a conclusion. Good lawyers exercise judgment, and good exam answers should demonstrate that the student can exercise judgment too. While many exams may have more than one reasonable "right answer," professors want you to draw a conclusion and justify why you reach that conclusion. Thus, in its own paragraph after the application, have a one sentence conclusion on each topic. For example: "Thus, the defendant acted with intent." When you are done addressing each element, make sure you also provide a conclusion for the overarching topic. For example: "Defendant will be liable for assault."

Other Considerations

A. Emphasize Policy

Law school exams are not primarily designed to test policy, or other esoteric arguments about law that you may have discussed in class. The bread and butter of most law school exams is to apply legal knowledge to a new set of facts. That said, the very best answers to law school exams incorporate policy considerations into the answer.

Demonstrate to your professor that you understand the nuance behind the law and that on close questions you recognize that the so-called black letter law never provides a clear answer. To do this, explain how policy considerations inform why you reach the conclusion you do.

B. Use Plain English

This is not the time for Shakespearean prose. You must write clearly. A sloppy exam with fragments or run-on sentences and many typographical and grammatical mistakes is difficult to read. Most professors will not grade on writing style; however, the best-written, most organized exams are often also the strongest substantive exams. Use plain English, and write short, easy-to-follow, declarative sentences.

Do not use abbreviations. An exam is time-pressured; still, you should write your answer in complete English. Do not use SMJ for subject matter jurisdiction. Do not use PJ for personal jurisdiction. Do not use PPB for principle place of business. Imagine reading 100 exams that say P does not have SMJ or PJ because D's PPB was not in State X. You are a lawyer. Write using complete words. There may be a few exceptions to this rule. If you professor tells you to abbreviate terms, follow your professor's instructions. Also, it is common to abbreviate Plaintiff as P and Defendant as D. As long as those are your only abbreviations you may get away with it. You should check with your professor first. Also, although you are using "IRAC," do not label the different parts of your analysis with I, R, A, and C.

C. Use Specific Facts

Although you need to use plain English, do not over-simplify or generalize the facts when making your arguments. Be specific. Assume the facts of your exam state: Vanessa told Ahmad, "I will pay $5,000 for your Honda Civic if you bring the car to my house tomorrow at noon." Don't summarize these facts in your argument by stating there was an offer because Vanessa gave definite terms as to the price, good to be sold, timing, and location of the sale. Rather, state that Vanessa provided definite terms because Vanessa offered $5,000 as the price, specified Ahmad's Honda Civic as the good, stated the location of the sale as her house, and stated the time of the sale at noon. Use specific facts in your argument. It will help you stay accurate in your analysis and help you avoid over-generalizing the issues.

D. Write Enough

A common blunder for new students is to underestimate how much a student must write to do well on a law school essay exam. The longest answers certainly are not the best, but very short answers rarely are able to sufficiently address the issues raised in the exam. A student who turns in one or two double-spaced pages in response to an hour-long essay exam is almost certainly guaranteeing themselves a poor (perhaps failing) grade.

Although very short answers will not do well, precision and economy matter. Long-rambling answers invariably do poorly. The student who madly "vomits on the page" all information they know about the course is guaranteed a mediocre grade. Strong exam answers are lean and focused, with every word included for a reason.

E. Avoid Humor

As a general rule, using humor in your exam answer is almost always a mistake. The professor takes the exam questions seriously and grades the exams seriously — you should take it seriously too. Humor is rarely appropriate. This is not the time to be funny or sarcastic. Humor in an exam does not earn you any additional points. At best, all it does is waste valuable time. At worst, it could hurt you and oftentimes seems strained.

F. Use Common Sense

Don't forget common sense. You don't want to become an automaton, flooding your exam answers with canned nonsense that leads to ridiculous results. Keep your common sense and gut instincts. If you conclude that the court should strike as unconstitutional some long-standing (and previously unchallenged) law, or that a court should punish some innocuous activity with years of imprisonment, or your conclusion would lead to societal chaos and cause mass disruption, you should pause (at least for a moment). The very best law students don't toss their judgment aside at the exam door.

A side note about common sense: if your professor tells you to write in a certain way on the exam, do what your professor tells you to do. Even if it is not IRAC. Even if all of your other professors instruct you differently. Even if your professor's instructions conflict with your prior experience with organization or exam taking. Your professor is the one grading your exam. Follow your professor's instructions.

Learning by Example

Let me give you an example to illustrate the difference between a weak and a strong exam answer. Assume defendant drove into plaintiff's car on a busy street while the defendant was both speeding and talking on his cell phone. The accident injured both the plaintiff and the defendant, and they were taken to a local hospital.

Several hours later, the plaintiff saw the defendant in the hospital. In front of several doctors, the plaintiff punched the defendant in the nose screaming, "I can't believe you ruined my new car!" Plaintiff sued the defendant for negligence, seeking damages for the injuries to herself and to her car resulting from the accident. Defendant plans to sue plaintiff in return for damages to himself resulting from the punch.

Assume one of the questions asked on the exam is whether the defendant's claim against plaintiff for punching him is a compulsory counterclaim. A compulsory counterclaim is a claim that must be raised in the defendant's response to plaintiff's lawsuit or it is waived. A claim is compulsory if it arises from the "same transaction or occurrence" as the underlying claim. In determining whether claims arise from the "same transaction or occurrence," courts usually ask whether there exists a logical relationship between the two claims where separate trials on each of the claims would involve a substantial duplication of effort and time by the parties and the courts.

Here are four sample answers to this issue.

Exam Answer #1

The defendant's claim is a probably a compulsory counterclaim. I think the two claims are connected to one another. Defendant may disagree and say, *inter alia*, that the claims are not logically connected, and a judge might agree with the defendant. But it's unlikely. Clearly in the case at bar this is compulsory counterclaim.

This answer is worth almost no points. It says nothing. Absolutely nothing. It doesn't directly tell you what the legal issue is, nor does it set forth a rule summary, and it doesn't apply the rules to the facts. The legal rule that the student uses is incorrect ("connected" instead of "logical relationship"). Worse yet, the student uses legalese in an attempt to sound lawyerly, without saying anything ("inter alia," "the case at bar"). Nowhere does the student provide a reason for the conclusion. The use of the word "clearly" is also a mistake. A clear answer does not exist. The fact the student thinks there is one betrays the student's misunderstanding of the law.

Exam Answer #2

The issue is whether the defendant's claim is a compulsory counterclaim because it arose from the same transaction or occurrence as the plaintiff's negligence claim. Compulsory counterclaims are governed under Rule 13 of the Federal Rules of Civil Procedure. In class, we talked about the history behind and purpose behind compulsory counterclaims. Requiring that compulsory counterclaims be brought in one suit makes a great deal of sense because courts are congested, and it's very costly to have separate trials on a whole bunch of issues. And if you're a judge you'd want to hear the same case only once. This is the point Justice Brennan made in the case we read.

Compulsory counterclaims are also what the *Smith* case talks about in detail. In that case, the court found that compulsory counterclaims are claims that arise from the same transaction or occurrence. The court found that a defamation claim did not arise out of the same events as a negligence claim. There was a dissent that disagreed, but the majority found the defamation claim was not a compulsory counterclaim. (Professor, you said the same thing in class — compulsory counterclaims arise from the same transaction or occurrence.)

This is a close call (And reasonable minds can differ.) But I think the court would likely find they arose from the same event (i.e., the car accident). It certainly would be better to have one trial than two here. It's exactly what the *Smith* case said.

Side note, thanks professor for a great class this semester!

This is worse. Although this student sets out a rule summary (sort of), they don't apply the rules to the facts of this case. No analysis exists at all. The writer only draws a conclusion — this is not legal analysis.

Don't let the long answer fool you. This tells you even less than the prior answer. The example is the "tell-you-everything-I-know-about-the-class" approach that may have served students well in college, but will earn you very low grades in law school. The student talks a lot about counterclaims in general, but does not spend much time explaining why there is or is not a compulsory counterclaim in this particular case. The student does not answer the question asked. Finally, the attempt to curry favor at the end will annoy many professors.

Exam Answer #3

The issue is whether the defendant's claim is a compulsory counterclaim.

Compulsory counterclaims are claims that arise from the same transaction or occurrence.

In this case, the claims arise from the same transaction because they both have to do with the car accident. In determining whether claims arise from the "same transaction or occurrence," courts ask if a logical relationship exists between the two claims where separate trials on each of the claims would involve a substantial duplication of effort and time by the parties and the courts. Here, they seem to have a logical relationship because plaintiff punched defendant as a result of the accident.

Therefore, the court will likely find the assault claim to be compulsory.

Okay, this is better. Perhaps an average or perhaps slightly below average answer. The student starts off by identifying the legal issue and then sets out an accurate rule. The student falls short though in at least two ways. First, organization. Notice that the student first brings up the rule regarding logical relationship in the application part of the answer. All relevant rules should be set forth together in the "rule" paragraph. Avoid introducing new rules in your arguments. Second, the factual analysis is minimal and conclusory. The student discusses only two facts (that the claims have to do with the car accident, and that "plaintiff punched defendant because of the accident"). The student fails to acknowledge any nuance in the answer and does not note plausible counter-arguments.

Exam Answer #4

1. Is the Defendant's Claim a Compulsory Counterclaim?

Compulsory counterclaims are claims against opposing parties that arise from the same transaction or occurrence. In determining this, courts ask if a logical relationship exists between the two claims where separate trials on each of the claims would involve a substantial duplication of effort and time by the parties and the courts.

Here, one side could argue that the defendant's claim is not a compulsory counterclaim. The events did not arise from the same transaction or occurrence *because* the punching occurred at a different place than the accident — hospital, rather than busy street — and the punching occurred at a different time — several hours later. The two cases also involved different witnesses. For the car accident, the witnesses are those on the street. For the punching incident, the witnesses are the doctors. Furthermore, the evidence in the negligence case would involve whether the defendant was speeding or talking on his cell phone, while the punching claim would focus on what the plaintiff did in the hospital. As the evidence and witnesses will be different, substantial duplication of effort and time would not occur if the claims were heard separately.

These arguments are likely to fail. It is more likely that the two claims arose from the same transaction or occurrence *because* the two events occurred at approximately the same time — the accident occurred only a few hours earlier than the punching — and the two claims both involved the same event — the car accident. If the car accident had not occurred, the plaintiff and defendant would not have been in the hospital and the plaintiff would not have punched defendant in the nose. Furthermore, the facts say the reason the plaintiff punched the defendant was because the defendant "ruined his car." Finally, the parties to both claims are the same. The overlap of the parties and topic of the car accident creates a logical relationship between the two events so that it would make sense for a jury to hear the two claims together. Although it is a close call, given the increasing congestion in courts and the perception that too many lawsuits are filed, a judge may be more likely to find that the two claims must be brought together and that the assault claim is compulsory.

Thus, the defendant's claim is a compulsory counter-claim.

Finally, here's a strong answer. I would give it an A. It starts with a clear heading that identifies the issue. The issue is followed by a precise and correct rule summary. The rule summary identifies the rules (same transaction or occurrence, logical relationship) and the reason for the rule (avoids duplication). It is even organized beautifully as the rules are all in one paragraph together before the analysis begins. The analysis is also well thought-out and thorough. The analysis points to specific facts to explain why the student concludes that claims are logically related and includes a counter-argument. The student also touches on a policy implication — the congestion in the courts, and then ends with a conclusion.

Emergencies and After the Exam

If you have studied, kept up with class throughout the semester and taken practice exams, you'll do fine. However, what happens in situations when things don't go fine....

A. If Your Mind Blanks

Often essay exams will have more than one question (or at least several calls of the question). What should you do if your mind simply goes blank and you don't understand what is being asked, or if you have no idea how to answer the question?

In these situations, the most important thing is not to panic. Take a deep breath. And then take another. After you've done that, look at the call of the question again, and in your mind go through a checklist of the main topics covered in the course. Do any of them apply? Often going through the outline of topics in your mind will help you hit upon what the professor is asking.

If after a few minutes, you still have no idea — move on. Go onto the next essay question. Don't waste more time. You can always go back. Moving on will reduce your anxiety and it may well be that the second question is easier to answer. After answering another question, when you return you may well see the question in a new light.

B. If All Else Fails

Sometimes, however, no matter how well prepared you are, you might have a "freak-out" moment and can't spot any issues on the exam. This rarely happens for students who have prepared properly. Students who are prepared usually will understand what the professor is looking for. But what happens if you can't understand the first question, and after flipping to the second you don't understand it either? The entire exam is now reading like a foreign language. Even after taking some deep breaths and some time to reflect, you have no idea what to do.

You've been whipped into a frenzy and are tempted to run from the exam room screaming pulling out your hair as you go. You suspect, however, that doing so may guarantee you a failing grade, not to mention a special place in the school's urban legends for years to come.

If all else fails, start going through the main topics or legal issues covered in the course and write short IRACs, applying the facts of the question, to each topic. There's two reasons for doing this. First, after writing out several topics, you may hit upon an issue that actually is relevant to the question or otherwise spurs you to spot analysis the professor is looking for. Sometimes just writing will calm you down and allow you to focus and pass the "freak-out" moment. Second, at least you're giving the professor something. If you turn in an exam with no writing, the professor has no choice but to give you a failing grade. If you write out the main topics covered in the class the professor may take mercy and give you some sympathy points that will pull you above the passing line.

C. A Few Nevers

Two absolute "nevers" after law school exams. First, never talk about the substantive aspects of the exam with your friends after the exam is over. It's done. Move on. It's time to focus on the next exam. Talking about the exam will only increase your anxiety as you discover issues that you may have missed. What's worse is you may not have missed the issue at all — it may be that your friend misread the question. But you'll never know. By talking with friends, you guarantee stressing yourself out. Keep the discussion generic (e.g., "that was a tough exam!").

Second, whatever you do, do not call or email your professor to discuss how you did on the exam before the professors submits the course grades. Contacting your professor is unprofessional. Usually professors grade anonymously. Providing a professor with any information about how you answered the exam question destroys that anonymity.

Another point. How well you performed on an exam is nearly impossible to predict. For most schools, law school grades are curved. You receive a grade not on how well you did in absolute terms, but on how well you did relative to your classmates. Your grade, therefore, will not necessarily correlate to how well you thought you performed. If an exam felt particularly difficult, don't be surprised if you scored very well. It may mean that you were just less lost on the exam than your classmates. Similarly, you may not do as well on an exam that you thought was quite easy — it may have been easy for all your classmates too.

D. Self-Assessment

At some point you will receive your grade and your exam will usually be available to you. Many students never collect their exams — you should. After each exam, retrieve the exam and assess what you did well and what you didn't do well. If the professor has provided a cut sheet or an answer key, this should be fairly easy to do. If the professor has not provided a cut sheet or answer key, then consider making an appointment to see the professor. This is not the time to grade-grub (i.e., never argue that you should have received a higher grade), but asking the professor for insight into how you could have done better is appropriate.

E. Final Words on Exams and Grades

A common question students ask is how important are law school grades? In the short term, first-year grades can be very important. The stakes are high. Employers need an easy way to assess potential applicants, and grades are considered an easy proxy for your potential as a lawyer. If your goal is to work in a very large, so-called elite law-firm, grades for most law schools are critical to getting your foot in the door. A slate of straight A's is also probably necessary to have any chance to clerk for a federal appellate court or the U.S. Supreme Court. There's your pride too. There's something unsettling when you find out you didn't do as well as the irritating schlub in the front row who flubbed every question asked when called on in class.

However, keep in mind law school grades are probably also much less important than many think. First, your law school GPA is often completely irrelevant after your first job. Once you have graduated, employers are much more concerned with whether you are a good attorney than what your law school GPA was. Second, for most law students at most law schools, jobs are obtained through networking and alumni connections. In those circumstances, while strong grades are helpful, other criteria often comes into play. Third, grades may be key to obtaining a screening interview, but after that your ability to interview in a professional way and your personality is substantially more important. Plenty of stories exist of the very top student with the highest grades struggling to obtain a job because of social awkwardness or an inability to interview well.

_____

That's it. That's all the advice I have. Follow it and you'll do fine.

Checklist Reminders

Preparing for Final Exams

- ❑ Know the exam details (is it open, closed, how many questions, how long…)
- ❑ Read the school's exam rules (what can you bring into the exam)
- ❑ Review prior exams given by professor
- ❑ Keep outlines updated on a weekly basis
- ❑ Schedule practice exams early and often (don't wait until the end of the semester!)
- ❑ Take some practice exams under timed conditions
- ❑ Learn how professor grades for each course
- ❑ Go to any review sessions
- ❑ Take advantage of Academic Support
- ❑ Learn the law (rule summaries) by heart

The Day of the Exam

- ❑ Arrive early
- ❑ Arrive prepared (pens, pencils, highlighters, pencil sharpeners, erasers, analog clock, snacks, if permitted)
- ❑ Don't cram
- ❑ Dress in layers and comfortably
- ❑ Test laptop before exam to ensure it's working properly

Starting the Exam

- ❑ Read the exam instructions carefully
- ❑ Allocate time among question
- ❑ Read the call of the question
- ❑ Read the facts carefully (a few times)
- ❑ Outline the answer

Writing the Exam

- ❑ Stay calm and breathe

- ❑ *No preambles — answer the question asked. Get right to it!*
- ❑ *Use headings*
- ❑ *Use IRAC (rules before analysis)*
- ❑ *Write precise, succinct rules*
- ❑ *Use the facts (all of them)*
- ❑ *Explain conclusions and significance of facts (use the word "because")*
- ❑ *Argue both sides*
- ❑ *Emphasize policy considerations*
- ❑ *Write clearly and legibly*
- ❑ *Don't use humor (be professional)*
- ❑ *Use common sense (watch out for crazy conclusions!)*

After the Exam

- ❑ *Don't talk about the exam's substance right after the exam (no exam debrief with friends)*
- ❑ *Don't pester the professor*
- ❑ *Pick up exams after they are graded*
- ❑ *Do a self-assessment after you receive your grade (how could you have improved)*
- ❑ *Visit professor for guidance, but no grade-grubbing!*
- ❑ *Keep it all in perspective*

7

LEGAL WRITING

Let me start with a boost of confidence: anyone can be a successful legal writer, even those of you who have floundered in your previous writing courses. In fact, I hate to burst any bubbles, but it is often the self-proclaimed "good-writers" who tend to struggle the most in this course. So for those of you who think this class is going to be a walk in the park, I've got some news for you. Legal writing is different from all other types of writing. Legal writing is structured. Very. When done properly, it is almost tediously formulaic. To those who truly understand it, legal writing is beautiful.

Lawyers are required to write using a prescribed formula. Until you master the formula, writing within it will feel uncomfortable and awkward. Learn to accept the discomfort if you want to succeed. Resist any inclination you may have to ignore the formula because "you know better." Hopefully, as you learn the formula, you will also learn to love it, or at least appreciate its structure.

The Basics

Let's start with some basic pointers about your legal writing course.

A. Objective v. Persuasive Writing

Most legal writing courses are split into two categories. In the fall semester, the course will focus on objective writing. In the spring semester, the course will focus on persuasive writing. Let's talk about each.

In the fall semester, you will write an objective memorandum. An objective memorandum is exactly that: objective. It is not biased. It does not take a side. The purpose of an objective memorandum is to (i) predict what a court is likely to rule on a particular set of facts and (ii) provide the reader a balanced discussion of the arguments for each side. When assigned to write an objective memorandum as a lawyer, remember it is an internal document. No one will see this document other than you, the attorneys in your law firm, and, possibly, your own client. So, be honest. Your supervising attorney is relying on your prediction to determine whether the firm should take on the client. Your supervising attorney is relying on your arguments when he or she goes to negotiate a settlement. If you down-play the opposing side's arguments, your supervising attorney will be at a disadvantage at the negotiation table. In some cases, your clients are also relying on your memorandum to make important decisions. They need to have the most accurate picture of the potential legal consequences of the considered actions. Thus, it must be objective and provide a fair analysis of the issues.

In the spring semester, you will learn how to write persuasively. You will be asked to draft a document in favor of your client with the purpose of persuading the court to take a particular action. The name of the document your professor assigns will vary, but it is often referred to as a persuasive brief. This is not same type of case brief discussed in Chapter 3 of this book. The case brief discussed earlier in Chapter 3 is a summary of one case designed to be a study tool for class. A persuasive brief is a formal document addressed to the court. A persuasive brief is not a balanced prediction, but takes a side and presents arguments in support of that side. To be effective, a persuasive brief will also refute counter-arguments. During the spring semester of your legal writing class, you will learn specific persuasive techniques to help you draft your brief persuasively.

B. Legal Writing Is Formulaic

Whether you are writing an objective memorandum or a persuasive brief, you will need to write using a specific legal writing formula. To be successful in your legal writing course, you need to follow the formula carefully. Pretend it is a science experiment and if you miss one step, your experiment will not work. If you miss a step in the legal writing formula, your end product will not earn you the grade you seek.

For all the excellent writers reading this book who are thinking, "I do not need the formula," or "I can write better without one," remember what

I said above: resist the temptation to think you know better. Do not debate whether the formula is effective. Even if you learned to write differently in the past, or believe the quality of your writing is nearly Dickensian in its brilliance, you need to let the past go and accept that legal writing is different. You need to buy-in fully and trust the system in order to be successful.

C. Legal Writing Is Simple and Concise

Hereafter. Therein. Shall. De facto. Inter alia. All words you should never include in your legal writing. Legal writing is simple and concise. Lawyers are busy. Judges are busy. Your job is to communicate the law and the relevant legal arguments as simply and concisely as possible so your supervisor and/or the judge reading your writing will be able to understand it on a first read. Don't try to use big words. Don't add in extra adjectives. Only use exactly what is necessary to understand your point. The simpler the language, the better.

Don't take my word for it. Try it yourself. Pretend you are a partner in a law firm and have twenty case files on your desk. You are busy trying to get through each one by the end of the day, and your associate pops into your office with a summary of a case you asked her to write up. Which of the two following case summaries would you prefer to read? Which would you understand more quickly?

Example 1: In *Trejo v. Johnson & Johnson*, the plaintiff was treated for an irregular skin syndrome caused by an allergic reaction after ingesting the non-prescription drug Motrin, which is used 100 million times a year in the United States. As a result of the plaintiff's allergic reaction to the medicine, the patient suffered from several ailments, including rashes, blisters, and wounds to the plaintiff's physique and limbs. The court held the plaintiff's claims were not effective circumstances for the consumer expectation test and the test was thus inapplicable to plaintiff's cause of action for design defect. The court held this because the plaintiff's claim was driven by medicinal aspects of an individual's particular sensitivity to various substances and contracting SJS/TEN was an idiosyncratic reaction to the medication.

Do you understand *Trejo* after reading this summary? The summary of the case above is accurate, but how many times would you have to read it to truly understand what happened in the case? Don't waste your time trying. Just read the next example and compare.

Example 2: In *Trejo v. Johnson & Johnson*, a patient took the over-the-counter medication Motrin. After taking the Motrin, the plaintiff contracted a rare skin disease and was hospitalized. The court held the consumer expectation test did not apply to the patient's case because the cause of the patient's disease was "complicated" and "technical." The court explained that the patient's disease was a result of an allergic reaction and allergic reactions are matters "driven by science." To apply the consumer expectation test, the jury would need to understand the science of why one person's body reacted to medication in a specific way. Thus, the case was a better fit to be tried under an alternative test.

Was that easier to follow? Why? Less words? Simpler words? More direct? Try to keep simplicity in mind as you enter into your legal writing course. Don't use a thesaurus. Use every day language. However, the use of simple language does not give you an excuse to become unprofessional or causal in your writing. Your language must still read like a serious document. Avoid contractions. Avoid first person. Avoid slang. Stay professional, but simple.

Learning the Formula

Let's walk through the legal writing formula that you will be required to follow so closely. The formula is commonly known as "CREAC." CREAC is an acronym that stands for Conclusion, Rule, Explanation, Application, and Conclusion. CREAC will be the legal formula for writing both objective memorandums in the fall and persuasive briefs in the spring.

For the purpose of illustrating each part of the formula, let's start with a short hypothetical. Assume you represent Sophie, who was charged with the illegal possession of narcotics. Sophie was visiting her friend's apartment when police came to the apartment to execute a warrant. While executing the warrant, the police searched Sophie's backpack and found narcotics. Assume you are asked by your supervising attorney to write an objective memorandum predicting whether the police's search of Sophie's backpack was permissible.

A. Conclusion

The first sentence in the legal formula is your conclusion. Your conclusion should set forth your ultimate conclusion on whether your client will win or lose on a specific issue. Was the search of Sophie's backpack permissible or not? Lawyers like to know your conclusion before they read your analysis. Thus, start your CREAC by stating your conclusion.

Note that the conclusion is specific to the parties and facts in your case. The conclusion for our hypothetical would state either: (i) The officers lawfully searched Sophie's backpack; or (ii) The officers unlawfully searched Sophia's backpack. It's that simple. One sentence.

B. Rule

After stating your conclusion, your paper should set forth the relevant law, or "rule," for the topic you are writing about. The rule portion of the formula is where you lay out the legal rules your reader should know in order to understand your analysis. Do not include a history of the rules or how they developed over time. Lawyers only need to know what the law is as it stands today. Do not include irrelevant parts of the law. Lawyers only need to know the legal rules that apply to the specific factual circumstances you were asked to write about.

When drafting your rule paragraph, you need to remember four basic principles. First, organize the rules from broad to specific. Second, connect the rules in a logical and accurate manner. Third, state the rules in present tense. Finally, quote key language from the rules. Let's look at some examples to illustrate each of these four principles.

1. Organize the Rules from Broad to Specific

Once you have found the relevant law for your paper, you need to set forth the rules in an organized manner. When organizing the rules that will be included in the rule paragraph, start with the broadest rules first. Next, set forth the more specific rules that further define those broad rules. Finally, end with the most specific sub-rules. Think of your rule paragraph as a funnel. The rules you begin with are broad, overarching background rules. As the paragraph continues, the rules become narrower. By the time you get to the end of the rule paragraph, the rules are the most specific sub-rules relevant to the paper. These specific sub-rules are the rules that are the most critical for your reader to know. The specific sub-rules are the ones that govern whether your client will win or lose. Look at the organization of the three rules in this paragraph:

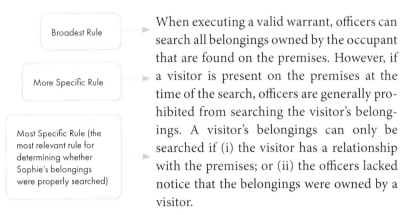

When executing a valid warrant, officers can search all belongings owned by the occupant that are found on the premises. However, if a visitor is present on the premises at the time of the search, officers are generally prohibited from searching the visitor's belongings. A visitor's belongings can only be searched if (i) the visitor has a relationship with the premises; or (ii) the officers lacked notice that the belongings were owned by a visitor.

The first rule starts with the general idea that officers can search all of the occupant's belongings. The next rule narrows that idea by setting forth the more specific rule that a visitor's belongings can generally not be searched. The final rule in the paragraph provides the most specific sub-rules setting forth the specific circumstances in which a visitor's belongings can be searched. It is this last sentence that is the most helpful in determining whether Sophie's backpack can be searched. The reader now knows that officers were permitted to search Sophie's backpack if either: (i) Sophie had a relationship with the apartment; or (ii) the officers were unaware that the backpack belonged to Sophie. The rule paragraph should always end with the most specific points that guide your reader as to who will win the case.

2. Connect Rules Logically and Accurately

The second principle in drafting your rule paragraph is to connect the rules logically and accurately, using appropriate transition words. After reading your rule paragraph, a reader should be able to understand the overall structure of the rule and how the pieces fit together. In order to achieve this goal, focus on the following: (i) connect your rules using the correct transition words, (ii) build language bridges between your sentences, and (iii) deliberately choose each word to maintain accuracy.

Transition words can assist you in connecting the ideas in your rule paragraph. It is essential that you choose transition words which accurately reflect the relationships between the rules. Poorly chosen transition words result in less clarity, rather than more. Let's use the rule paragraph from above to see the connections between each rule. We'll start with the first two rules set forth in that paragraph. Notice the effect of the transition word "however" in the second sentence:

> When executing a valid warrant, officers can search all containers owned by the occupant that are found on the premises. **However**, if a visitor is present on the premises at the time of the search, officers are generally prohibited from searching the visitor's belongings.

The transition word "however" lets your reader know the next rule is going to include something that contrasts with the first sentence. It immediately illustrates the rule will transition from what an officer can search to what an officer is prohibited from searching. Compare the following version of the two sentences using the word "Moreover" instead of "However."

> When executing a valid warrant, officers can search all belongings owned by the occupant that are found on the premises. **Moreover**, if a visitor is present on the premises at the time of the search, officers are generally prohibited from searching the visitor's belongings.

"Moreover" suggests the next rule will further support the first idea. "Moreover" suggests there will be another thing officers can search. That is not accurate so the transition word confuses your reader. Using the correct transition word is critical in making the connection between the two rules clear.

To connect the rules, you should also build language bridges between your sentences. Use the same language from one sentence in the sentence that follows. Look at the bolded words in these two sentences and notice how the language bridges the ideas together:

> If a visitor is present on the premises at the time of the search, officers are generally prohibited from **searching the visitor's belongings**. A **visitor's belongings can only be searched** if (i) the visitor has a relationship with the premises; or (ii) the officer's lacked noticed that the belongings were owned by a visitor.

By beginning the second sentence with the same terminology used in the first sentence, your reader knows exactly what part of the rule the sentence is connected to. It makes the rules easier for a reader to follow and understand.

Finally, to connect the rules, you must be deliberate in your word choice. For example, in the legal world, the difference between "and," "or," "may," "shall," "must," and "consider" can be enormous in a legal rule. These small words can have a huge impact on the meaning of a rule and whether a party can win or lose the case. Compare these two rules:

- A visitor's belongings can only be searched if (i) the visitor has a relationship with the premises; **or** (ii) the officer's lacked notice that the belongings were owned by a visitor.
- An officer can search a visitor's belongings if the visitor has a relationship to the premises. In order to search a visitor's belongings, an officer **must** also lack notice that the belongings were owned by a visitor.

These two rules set forth very different requirements. According to the first rule, the officers were permitted to search Sophie's backpack if either Sophie had a relationship with the apartment or if the officers were unaware the backpack belonged to Sophie. Thus, the officers could actually know the backpack was Sophie's, know Sophie is a visitor, and still lawfully search her backpack as long as she has a relationship with the premises.

Pursuant to the second rule, an officer is permitted to search Sophie's backpack only if Sophie has a relationship with the premises AND the officers were unaware the backpack belonged to Sophie. Under this rule, Sophie will automatically win the case if the officers knew she was a visitor and knew the backpack belonged to her.

In drafting your rule, remember to use the correct transition words, build language bridges between your sentences, and deliberately choose each word as you set forth your rules.

3. State the Rules in Present Tense

The third principle in drafting your rule paragraph is to draft the rules in present tense. Rules are ongoing principles that will be applied to future cases. Thus, the wording should be: "Officers can **search** a visitor's belongings if the visitor **has** a relationship with the premises." The rule should not be stated as: "An officer **searched** the visitor's belongings because the visitor **had** a relationship with the premises."

4. Quote Key Language from the Rules

The exact wording of the law is critical in analyzing a case. When you write a memorandum for your supervising attorney or write a persuasive brief for the court, your audience will want to know the exact wording of the rule. Thus, it is critical to quote the key language from your rules. Here is an example of a rule quoting just the key language:

> When executing a valid warrant, officers can search "all belongings owned by the occupant that are found on the premises."

Notice just a select part of the sentence is quoted. Avoid quoting the entire sentences in your legal writing. Rather, incorporate the key part of the quote into your own sentence and quote just the language you want your reader to focus on. Within the rule paragraph, several of your sentences may contain part of a quote; however, you should not quote in every sentence. Select your quotations sparingly. Using quotation marks is like bolding or italicizing for emphasis. If you bold every sentence in the paragraph, the bolding loses its effect. Quote only the key parts of the language you want your reader to remember.

C. Explanation

The next part of the formula is called the explanation of the law. In this explanation part of the formula, you will "explain" in more detail the specific sub-rules you ended with in your rule paragraph. You explain these sub-rules by summarizing prior cases where the court applied the sub-rules to different factual scenarios. The explanation is typically broken down into multiple paragraphs, so the first step in drafting the explanation is deciding what topic each paragraph will discuss. The next step is to draft each of those paragraphs. Let's take these two ideas in turn.

1. Topics for Your Explanation Paragraphs

Your explanation section of the paper will break down into different paragraphs: one paragraph for each topic you need to explain. The topics should be legal topics — specific sub-rules that your reader needs to learn more about. So, the first step in drafting the explanation is to decide how many different sub-rules need to be explained.

In choosing the sub-rules that need to be explained, look back to the end of your rule paragraph. If you have drafted the rule paragraph correctly, the paragraph should end with the most specific sub-rules that are critical to predicting whether a party will win or lose the case. Look at these specific sub-rules and decide how many sub-parts the rule naturally breaks into. In our rule paragraph above, we ended with this sub-rule:

> A visitor's belongings can only be searched if (i) the visitor has a relationship with the premises; or (ii) the officer's lacked noticed that the belongings were owned by a visitor.

This sub-rule naturally breaks down into two parts. First, when a visitor has a relationship with the premises. Second, when officers have notice that belongings are owned by a visitor. Under this rule, your explanation would break into two paragraphs. One paragraph would illustrate cases when a visitor had a relationship with the premises and the second paragraph would illustrate when officers have notice that belongings are owned by a visitor.

2. Drafting Explanation Paragraphs

Once you know how many different legal topics you will explain in your paper, you are ready to draft the paragraphs. Each explanation paragraph has two parts: (i) a thesis statement; and (ii) case illustrations.

i. Thesis Statements

Your thesis statement should state the sub-rule you are illustrating in that paragraph and provide critical details about that sub-rule. The thesis is often one sentence, but can also be two, or even three sentences. The goal of the thesis statement is to provide the reader the main point you will be addressing in the paragraph and provide the relevant details about the sub-rule that you want your reader to remember. Here is an example of thesis sentences you could include in the explanation section:

> Thesis #1: **A visitor's belongings can be searched if** the visitor has a relationship to the premises. A visitor has a relationship to the

premises if the visitor is present during criminal activity or if the visitor's presence is more than temporary.

Thesis #2: Alternatively, **a visitor's belongings can be searched if** the officers lacked notice that the belongings were owned by the visitor. The location of the belongings and markings on the belongings can provide constructive notice that an item belongs to a visitor.

Notice the consistency in language between the two thesis sentences. If your thesis sentences are drafted properly, they should flow well together and use consistent language. Also, notice the additional details about the rule that are added to each thesis statement. These details come from the cases you will illustrate next within each paragraph. Look for these details in the "reasoning" part of each case and, if they help further define the rule, pull them into your thesis. Finally, notice the two thesis statements are written in present tense. Thesis sentences are rules, so they should be stated in the present tense.

ii. Case Illustrations

After each thesis statement, you should include 2–4 case illustrations to explain how the rule has been applied in the past (unless there is only one case that supports the thesis statement, in which case include only that one case as an illustration). Each case should be illustrated by setting forth the facts of the case, the holding of the case, and the reasoning of the case.

Facts: When drafting the facts of the case, include only the facts relevant to the specific topic of that paragraph. If you are drafting a paragraph about when someone has a relationship with the premises, include facts that illustrate the plaintiff's relationship with the premises. Facts that might be relevant include why the plaintiff was at the premises, how long the plaintiff planned to stay, how the plaintiff knew the occupants, etc. Do not include facts about the appearance of the item that was searched or the location of the item searched. A description of what the item looked like might relate to whether the officer knew the item was owned by a visitor, but it is not relevant to the visitor's relationship with the premises. Next, when drafting the relevant facts, draft them in past tense because the case already happened. Finally, when drafting the facts, do not refer to the parties in the case by name. Rather, refer to them by general characterization (employee, employer, owner, visitor, etc.).

Holding: After drafting the facts of the case, state the court's holding from the case. The holding should be the court's answer on the issue you are addressing in that CREAC. If your CREAC is discussing when a visitor's belongings can be lawfully searched, the holding should be whether the visitor's belongings in that specific case were searched lawfully. State the holding in past tense, and use the actual word "held."

Reasoning: After you state the court's holding, include the court's reasoning for its decision. Include only the reasoning relevant to the topic you are addressing. If you are drafting a case illustration for relationship, do not include the court's reasoning regarding why an officer would have notice the item was owned by a visitor. Rather, include the reasons why the visitor had or did not have a relationship with the premises. Make sure to include all relevant reasoning. In choosing which reasoning is relevant, think about the arguments that could be made about your own client's case. If either you or the opposing side would find part of the reasoning relevant to an argument about why Sophia had a relationship with the premises, you should include that part of the court's reasoning in the case illustration. Remember, the reasoning should directly connect back to the topic for that paragraph. If your thesis is about relationship, the reasoning part of the case illustration should be about relationship. When drafting the reasoning, you also should quote key language you want your reader to remember.

Here is an example of a complete explanation paragraph on the topic of relationship:

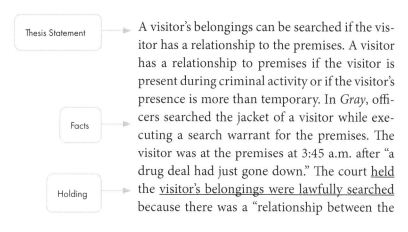

Thesis Statement → A visitor's belongings can be searched if the visitor has a relationship to the premises. A visitor has a relationship to premises if the visitor is present during criminal activity or if the visitor's presence is more than temporary. In *Gray*, officers searched the jacket of a visitor while executing a search warrant for the premises. The

Facts → visitor was at the premises at 3:45 a.m. after "a drug deal had just gone down." The court held

Holding → the visitor's belongings were lawfully searched because there was a "relationship between the person and the place." The court explained the visitor was not "a casual afternoon visitor to the premises," but was at the premises "at an unusual hour during criminal activity." The circumstances thus suggested he was more than a "mere visitor or passerby." Similarly, in *Giwa*, the officers properly searched a visitor's belongings who was spending the night at the premises. The defendant was alone at the premises and answered the door "clad only in a bathrobe and slacks." The court <u>held the visitor's belongings were properly searched</u> because he had "more than just a temporary presence in the apartment."

Reasoning

Facts

Holding

Reasoning

That's it. We have drafted one of our two explanation paragraphs. Repeat the same components for your explanation paragraph regarding when an officer has notice that an item belonged to a visitor. Both paragraphs together will complete your Explanation.

Notice that the facts of your client's case (Sophia's facts) never come up anywhere in the rule section of the CREAC or the explanation section of the CREAC. These two parts of the CREAC formula include only the relevant law. Your legal reader wants to learn everything relevant about the law before hearing any your arguments about your client's facts.

Also, note that one case can be used multiple times in several different explanation paragraphs. Your explanation paragraphs are organized by topic, not by case. Thus, if one case discusses two different topics, the case could be used in two different explanation paragraphs. Applying this to our example above, assume the *Gray* decision discusses both whether the defendant had a relationship to the premises and whether the officers had notice that the defendant was a visitor. *Gray* could then be discussed in your explanation paragraph on relationship and *Gray* could be discussed again in your explanation paragraph on notice. For each of these explanation paragraphs, only the portion of *Gray* that is relevant to the specific topic will be introduced. In the paragraph about relationship, only the facts, holding, and reasoning relevant to relationship will be discussed. In the paragraph about notice, only the facts, holding, and reasoning relevant to notice will be discussed.

D. Application

Now the fun part. The reason you came to law school. Time to make arguments! After explaining the relevant law, the next step in the CREAC formula is to apply the laws to your client's facts. This section of the formula is thus called the "application" of the law.

1. How to Make a Legal Argument

The American legal system is based on case precedent. Courts are bound to follow the rulings from prior court decisions. Thus, to win in court, an attorney must show a client's case is either similar to the facts of a previous case (and thus the court should reach the same decision as in that case), or different from the facts of a previous case (and thus the court should reach a different decision as in that case). An argument based on a comparison between the facts of previous case law and the client's facts is called an analogical argument. A complete analogical argument includes not only the comparison of facts, but also an explanation that further develops the ideas set forth in the comparison. The explanation should include additional facts from the client's case and apply the reasoning from prior case law.

Here is an example of an analogical argument from the prosecution's perspective. In this argument, the prosecution is arguing Sophie had a relationship with the apartment:

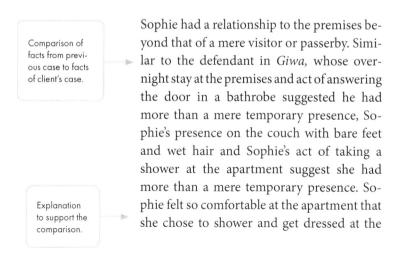

Comparison of facts from previous case to facts of client's case.

Explanation to support the comparison.

Sophie had a relationship to the premises beyond that of a mere visitor or passerby. Similar to the defendant in *Giwa*, whose overnight stay at the premises and act of answering the door in a bathrobe suggested he had more than a mere temporary presence, Sophie's presence on the couch with bare feet and wet hair and Sophie's act of taking a shower at the apartment suggest she had more than a mere temporary presence. Sophie felt so comfortable at the apartment that she chose to shower and get dressed at the apartment in lieu of her own home. At the time the officers arrived, Sophie was stretched out on the couch, with wet hair, and her shoes off. Sophie was so comfortable with the apartment that she engaged in activities typically done only by occupants of a home. Thus, Sophie was more than a mere casual visitor or "passerby." Sophie had a relationship with the property.

Explanation to support the comparison.

In this example, the facts of Sophie's case (relaxing on the couch and showering at the apartment) are compared to the facts of the defendant in *Giwa* (spending the night and answering the door in a bathrobe). The attorney argues that because the facts in *Giwa* were enough for a relationship, the facts in Sophie's case are also enough to show a relationship. The attorney then explains the comparison and further develops the argument by bringing in additional facts and reasoning to support the comparison.

Here is an alternate example, this time from Sophie's perspective. In this argument, Sophie's attorneys are arguing Sophie did not have a relationship with the premises:

Sophie did not have a relationship with the apartment, but was merely a casual visitor passing by. Unlike the visitor in *Gray,* who was found at the premises at 3:45 a.m. in the middle of a drug bust, Sophie was merely visiting friends in the afternoon before a football game. There was nothing unusual about her visit that afternoon and the officers had no reason to believe she was involved in any criminal wrongdoing. Sophie was simply stopping by the apartment to take a shower and have a beer before heading to a football game. She planned to stay for a short time and was merely a casual visitor who planned a temporary visit to see her friends before heading to a game. She did not have a relationship with the apartment.

Comparison of facts from previous case to facts of client's case.

Explanation to support the comparison.

In this example, the facts of Sophie's case (at the apartment in the afternoon before a football game) are compared to the facts of the defendant in *Gray* (at the premises at 3:45 a.m. during a drug bust). Given the difference between these facts, the attorney argues the ruling in the case should be different than the ruling in *Gray*. In *Gray*, there was a relationship. Since Sophie's facts are different, the court should find there is not a relationship. The attorney then further explains the argument by bringing in additional facts and reasoning to support the comparison.

Although analogical arguments are the most common arguments made in legal writing, you are likely to encounter other types of legal arguments as well, including rule-based arguments and policy arguments. A rule-based argument directly applies the legal rule to the facts of your client's case without ever making an analogy to the facts of the case law. A policy argument applies the policy for the law to the client's facts. Policy is the reason why the law was passed. In the law of search warrants, the policy of requiring search warrants is to protect the privacy rights of citizens. A policy argument applies the reason behind the law to support a specific conclusion. You will learn more about these types of arguments from your legal writing professor.

Regardless of the type of legal argument you are making, make sure your arguments apply only law that you previously set forth in your Rule and Explanation sections of the formula. Avoid introducing new laws in the Application section that were not previously discussed in your CREAC.

2. How to Organize Your Arguments

Now that you know how to make a legal argument, let's talk about how to organize the legal arguments. The organization of your arguments will depend on what type of legal writing you are drafting. If you are drafting an objective memorandum, you will need to include strong arguments for both sides of the case and will have a section in the application for each side. If you are drafting a persuasive brief, you will organize your arguments solely around your own client's strongest points. There will not be a section that sets forth arguments for the opposing side. Let's dig a little deeper.

i. Organization for Objective Memorandum

In the fall semester, you will likely draft an objective memorandum. When writing an objective memorandum, your job is to provide an impartial and fair analysis of the case without taking a side. The application section will thus include strong arguments for both sides of the issue in question. The application section of an objective memorandum breaks into three parts: (a) initial arguments, (b) counter-arguments, and (c) rebuttal.

Initial Arguments: Start your application section with the arguments in favor of the party you predict will prevail in court. The prevailing party may be your client or the prevailing party may be the opposing side. Remember to predict who will win from an *objective* standpoint. When drafting the initial arguments, start with an overall conclusion for the side you predict will win. For example, if you think the prosecution will prevail in the search of Sophie's backpack, you would write: "The officers lawfully searched Sophie's backpack." After stating this conclusion, set forth the legal arguments in support of that conclusion. Include *all* relevant arguments in support of the conclusion. If there are two reasons why the search was lawful, set forth an argument for each of those two reasons: (i) make an argument why Sophie had a relationship; and (ii) make an argument why the officers lacked notice that the backpack was Sophie's.

Counter-Arguments: The next step in the application section is to set forth the arguments for the side you predict will lose in court. Start by stating the overall conclusion for the losing side. The conclusion should indicate to your reader the paper is transitioning to the counter-arguments. Here is an example of a conclusion that indicates you are transitioning to the counter-arguments: "Sophie may argue that the officers unlawfully searched her backpack." After stating the overall conclusion for the losing side, set forth the legal arguments in support of that conclusion. Remember to provide the strongest arguments possible for this "losing" side. Your attorney needs to know the strongest arguments for both sides, even if you decide the side will not ultimately prevail. Also, make sure to include *all* relevant arguments in support of the conclusion for this side. If there are two reasons why the search was unlawful, set forth an argument for each of those reasons: (i) make an argument why Sophie did not have a relationship to the premises; and (ii) make an argument why the officers should have known the backpack belonged to Sophie.

Rebuttal: The final step in the application is to rebut the counter-arguments. Start with a transition sentence letting your reader know you are transitioning into the rebuttal. For example, "Sophie's arguments will likely fail." After transitioning into your rebuttal, address each point raised in the counter-arguments and explain why it is not a strong enough argument to prevail. Once you complete the rebuttal, you are done with the Application.

ii. Organization for Persuasive Brief

In the spring semester, you will likely draft a persuasive brief. In a persuasive brief, you will be taking a side — your client's side. In the persuasive brief, you will anticipate and rebut counter-arguments, but you will not devote an entire section of your paper to making those arguments on behalf of the opposing side. Thus, the organization of your application will be different for this type of document.

In a persuasive brief, you should organize all of your arguments as initial arguments. Start with your overall conclusion and then argue each relevant point in support of that conclusion. Do not transition into a counter-argument section. Do not have a separate rebuttal section. Rather, anticipate what the opposing side may argue and affirmatively rebut those arguments as you make your own arguments.

An example will make this clearer. Assume you represent Sophie and you are drafting a persuasive brief to convince the court that Sophie's backpack was unlawfully searched. You anticipate the prosecution will argue Sophie had a relationship with the premises because Sophie took a shower at the apartment. Instead of creating a counter-argument section to set forth that argument, simply refute the argument as you make your own argument on why there was not a relationship:

> The search of Sophie's belongings was unlawful. First, Sophie did not have a relationship with the apartment. Unlike the visitor in *Gray,* who was found at the premises at 3:45 a.m. in the middle of a drug bust, Sophie was merely visiting friends in the afternoon on the way to a football game. There was nothing unusual about her visit and the officers had no reason to believe she was involved in any criminal wrongdoing. Rather, Sophie was simply stopping by the apartment to take a shower and have a beer before heading to a game. Sophie's decision to

shower at the premises does not take away her constitutional right to be free from unlawful search and seizure. The defendant's decision in *Giwa* to spend the night at the premises by himself made his relationship with the premises similar to that of an occupant and thus his belongings were justifiably searched. However, it is common for a college student to take a quick shower at a friend's house right before a football game and taking a shower does not equate her to an occupant of the premises. Sophie never spent the night at the apartment and was not alone at the apartment for any period of time. She chose to shower there exactly because she was in a hurry and did not have time to go home to change before the game. Thus, she was no more than a casual visitor who planned a temporary visit to see her friends.

> Addresses the counter-argument as part of Sophie's argument

Notice in this argument that the counter-argument about Sophie's shower is addressed and not ignored. However, it is not placed in its own paragraph and is only brought up in the context of why Sophie did not have a relationship with the apartment. The organization of your Application is different when writing a persuasive brief because there is not a separate section where the opponent's arguments are explained. Rather, the opposing arguments are addressed as part of your own client's arguments.

E. Conclusion

After completing your Application, conclude the formula by restating the overall conclusion you started with at the beginning of the CREAC. The conclusions act as bookends, with the same idea opening and closing the analysis.

One last note about this legal formula. Although many legal writing professors use the acronym CREAC, there are actually a variety of different names for it. Some legal writing professors call it CRAC, others call it CRuPAC, others may have their own specific acronym. Regardless of the name, the formula is the same. CRAC stands for Conclusion, Rule, Application, Conclusion. Under this acronym, the "Rule" includes both the rule paragraph and the explanation of those rules. CRuPAC stands for Conclusion, Rule, Proof, Application, Conclusion. The "Proof" part of this acronym is the same things as the "Explanation" in CREAC. Don't worry about what your professor calls the formula because it will all boil down to the same parts.

Organizing a Multi-Issue Paper

At this point, we have covered how to structure a paper that addresses a single legal issue. Hopefully you have learned to explain the law governing the legal issue first and then provide legal arguments for each side using the formula CREAC. Let's take it a step further and learn what to do if there is more than one relevant legal issue. Most legal problems involve several legal issues. When this occurs, you should draft one CREAC for each legal issue. The tough part, however, is determining how many relevant issues exist. It is not always obvious. To determine how many legal issues are at stake, you must understand the different types of legal tests that exist in the law. Once you know the legal test you are dealing with, you can determine how many CREACs you need and organize your paper accordingly.

A. Understanding Different Legal Tests

There are numerous types of legal tests. I will take you through the three most basic tests you will likely encounter as a first-year law student: (i) an elements test; (ii) a factors test; and (iii) a disjunctive test.

Let's start with an elements test. Elements are requirements: things that must be proven in order to win a case. If you are missing even one element, you lose the case. Assume your client is charged with murder and the prosecution has to prove two elements: (i) the defendant caused the victim's death; and (ii) the defendant intended to kill the victim. Perhaps the prosecution can prove your client killed the victim when your client hit the victim with his car. However, if your client veered off the road onto the sidewalk to avoid a child running into the street, the prosecution will lose the case because the prosecution will not be able to prove your client intended to kill the victim. The prosecution is missing one of the elements: intent. To win a case with elements, the attorney must prove all elements are met.

Let's move on to a factors test. Factors are not requirements. Factors are considerations: things the court weighs and thinks about when making a decision, but not necessary components to win the case. Take a legal test regarding child custody as an example. After a divorce, the court must determine whether a child will be placed with the mother or the father. In making its decision, the court considers the "best interests of the child," including (i) the financial stability of the parents; (ii) where other siblings are placed; (iii) any history of substance abuse by a parent; and (iv) the child's own wishes. To receive custody of a child, the parent does not have to show all of these things exist. Perhaps you represent the father and the father is not as financially stable as the child's mother. Perhaps the father even has a history of substance abuse. However, perhaps the father has recovered from his substance abuse problems, has custody of another sibling, and the child wishes to stay with the father. After considering all factors, a court may decide the best interests of the child are to stay with the father in spite of the history of substance abuse and in spite of the lack of financial resources. Alternatively, a court may decide the best interests of the child are to stay with the mother in spite of the placement of other siblings and in spite of the child's own wishes. In making a decision, the court will weigh all factors, but each factor is not an absolute requirement.

Finally, the disjunctive test. A disjunctive test provides two alternative ways to win. The plaintiff must prove one of two things. This is the type of test we have worked with when analyzing whether officers properly search Sophie's backpack. The search and seizure law we have used as an example thus far allows officers to search all containers found within the particular property if either (i) the visitor has a relationship with the premises; or (ii) the officers lacked notice that the container belonged to the visitor. Under this disjunctive test, the prosecution can win by proving either there was a relationship or the officers lacked notice. There are two alternative ways to win the case.

B. Tying Multiple CREACs Together

Once you determine the type of legal test you are working with, you need to break down the legal test to determine how many separate legal issues need to be addressed and decide whether those issues are best discussed independently in separate CREACs or together within one CREAC.

For an elements test, each element is independent of the other because the analysis of one element does not impact the analysis of a different element. Thus, if there are multiple elements, the general rule is to create one CREAC for each element. There are exceptions to this general rule and there may be occasions where two elements are so connected they need to be addressed within one CREAC. For now, remember the general rule is to draft one CREAC for each element.

A factors test and a disjunctive test, on the other hand, are typically analyzed within one CREAC. Factors are considerations made by the court to determine whether one requirement/element is met. Similarly, alternatives under a disjunctive are merely different ways to prove one requirement/element. Thus, many attorneys address factors within one CREAC and both alternatives within one CREAC. Again, there are exceptions to these general rules. The amount of discussion needed to explain one factor or one alternative may suggest addressing each factor or alternative in a separate CREAC. However, as a general rule, assume you will address all factors within one CREAC and both alternatives under a disjunctive test within one CREAC.

Ultimately, if your paper includes more than one CREAC, you must connect the CREACs together using an Overview Paragraph. The purpose of the overview is to introduce your reader to the legal test and set forth the different issues that will be addressed by each CREAC. An overview paragraph often includes your overall conclusion, a statement of the overarching legal test, policy, and a roadmap of the issues that will be discussed. Follow your professor's specific guidelines regarding what exactly to include in the overview paragraph.

Let's look at an example. If you are writing a memorandum on assault, and assault requires three separate elements, your paper will look like this:

Memorandum

Overview Paragraph: First, set forth your overall conclusion on whether the defendant committed an assault. Next, quote the exact wording of the legal test for assault. Next, include any relevant policy for why an individual is able to recover for assault. Finally, roadmap the specific elements that will be addressed in each of your CREACs. For example, an assault requires (i) an act by the defendant; (ii) intent to cause apprehension; and (iii) apprehension of harm by the victim.

1. Defendant's Act
   C: conclusion on whether the defendant acted
   R: rule regarding when something constitutes an act
   E: case examples of when a defendant acted in the past
   A: arguments regarding whether the defendant acted
   C: conclusion on whether the defendant acted

2. Intent to Cause Apprehension
   C: conclusion on whether the defendant intended to cause apprehension
   R: rule regarding when a defendant intends to cause apprehension
   E: case examples of when defendants have intended to cause apprehension in the past
   A: arguments regarding whether the defendant intended to cause apprehension
   C: conclusion on whether the defendant intended to cause apprehension

3. Apprehension of Harm by the Plaintiff
   C: conclusion on whether the victim suffered apprehension of harm
   R: rule regarding when a victim suffers apprehension of harm
   E: case examples of when victims have suffered apprehension of harm in the past
   A: arguments regarding whether the victim suffered apprehension of harm

C: conclusion on whether the victim suffered apprehension of harm

For this paper about assault, you would write three CREACs because there are three independent issues/elements. Notice that for each CREAC, the formula is tailored to one specific issue.

Final Words on Legal Writing

There are a few more aspects of writing that most first-year law students will encounter.

A. Ancillary Sections of a Memorandum or Brief

Although this chapter only walks you through the basic legal formula of CREAC, an objective memorandum also typically includes sections such as question presented, brief answer, and statement of facts. Similarly, a persuasive brief typically includes sections such as a table of contents, table of authorities, statement of the issues, introduction, and possibly a standard of review. These additional sections of the paper are ancillary to the main lessons you will focus on in your legal writing course. If you can master CREAC, these other pieces will fall right into place.

B. The Bluebook

The word "Bluebook" will soon become one of your most dreaded sounds. The Bluebook is a citation manual that sets forth the citation rules for legal documents. The rules are complex and take time to master. The examples of legal writing illustrated in this chapter do not include citations, but you can see an example of what a legal citation looks like in the example memorandum found in Appendix E. When you draft legal documents, almost every sentence in your rule and explanation paragraphs must be cited. After all, your paper is only convincing if it is based on actual authority you can cite to.

Although the Bluebook is intimidating at first glance, if you take one step at a time, learning the citation rules is manageable. The best way to master the Bluebook is to use the examples in the Bluebook as a guide to interpreting the rules. If a Bluebook citation rule is difficult to understand, look at the examples provided immediately after the rule and try to model your citation after the example.

C. Writing Style

Time to brush up on those commas. Semicolons, apostrophes, quotations, even colons — you will need them all. Your writing needs to be professional and it must be grammatically correct. You are expected to come to law school with an understanding of the basic grammar rules. There are some grammatical rules that legal writing professors commonly review, such as active voice and the use of nominalizations. However, for the most part, legal writing is not about learning grammar. You are expected to know it. If you have not practiced writing for a while or need some extra grammar help, think about finding a grammar app or online grammar subscription that works for you. There are plenty of programs that can help you brush up on the grammar rules and plenty of technology to check your legal writing papers for grammar errors. Take advantage of these resources. Many law schools also have a writing center that is designed to help students improve their writing style. If your school offers this service, take advantage of the writing center.

D. Legal Research

At some law schools, legal research is taught as a part of the legal writing course. At other law schools, legal research is taught as an independent course. Regardless of where you learn it, you will need to conduct legal research to find the relevant law to include into your memorandums or briefs. When conducting your research, there is one tip that can save you hours of work and several bottles of Advil: come up with a step-by-step research plan and follow it. Here is an example:

Step One: Read secondary sources to get a feel for the area of law and the type of test you will be working with. Secondary sources are not law themselves, but summarize the law in an organized and concise manner. The most commonly used secondary sources for legal research are called legal encyclopedias and practice guides. These secondary sources often reference relevant case names and/or statutes as they summarize the law so they are a great starting place for your research.

Step Two: Read the statutes and cases referenced in the secondary sources and read the relevant cases and/or statutes that are cited within those cases. This will give you a good base of cases to start with.

Step Three: The relevant cases you find will have topics/headnotes at the beginning of the case. The headnotes are a research tool that can be used to find other cases on the same topic. Find a few relevant headnotes/topics from your "base" of cases and research using those headnotes to find other relevant case law.

Step Four: By this point, you should have a good sense of what the law is and what the key cases are than govern the law. You are ready to take the next step: KeyCite or Shepardize the cases. By using this research tool, you can look for other cases that have cited to the ones you thought were helpful. You likely do not know what "KeyCite" or "Shepardize" mean, but do not worry. You will learn soon enough.

Step Five: Finally, after you have read numerous cases and have a good feel for what the law is and the terminology the court uses to describe the law, perform a word search to see if there are any cases you may have missed through these other methods. Hopefully many of the same cases you have already found show up in your search and you can feel good that your research plan worked. You may find one or two new cases to read by ending with this last step.

After you have completed these steps, stop researching. Legal research is daunting, and it is easy to get caught in a large forest looking for a small twig. You can spend hours researching a single issue and feel like the more you research, the more behind you are. You will rarely feel comfortable that you have found all relevant law and you will have an urge to continue researching endlessly. Recognize that these feelings are normal, but do something to overcome the feelings because you cannot research forever. If you have a research plan and follow it, you can feel confident in ending your research and you can start writing.

I'll leave you with my strongest advice on mastering legal writing: trust the process. Let go of everything you think you know about writing and have an open mind to learn a new approach. Even better, learn to love it. Those who enjoy what they do tend to perform better. If you are not a fan of writing, become one.

Checklist Reminders

The Basics

- ❑ *Be objective in the fall memorandum (provide a balanced discussion of the law and arguments)*

❑ *Follow the legal writing formula (even if it is different from how you learned to write)*

❑ *Use simple language in your writing and avoid legalese*

❑ *Write concisely*

The Formula

❑ *Start your CREAC by stating your conclusion*

❑ *Summarize the relevant law by stating your rules from broad to specific, ending in the most relevant legal rules to deciding the case.*

❑ *Organize your explanation of the law by legal topic, not by case*

❑ *For each explanation paragraph, include a thesis sentence and 2–4 case illustrations*

❑ *Draft your case illustrations by setting forth the relevant facts, holding, and reasoning*

❑ *In your application section, make analogical arguments followed by an explanation of your argument*

❑ *Organize your arguments in an objective memo by setting forth the pre-vailing arguments, counter-arguments, and rebuttal*

❑ *Organize your arguments in a persuasive brief by setting forth only your client's arguments (and incorporating responses to counter-arguments within them)*

❑ *End your CREAC by restating your conclusion*

Organizing a Multi-Issue Paper

❑ *Identify whether the legal test you are writing about is an elements test, factors test, or disjunctive test*

❑ *For each element identified, write one CREAC*

❑ *Tie multiple CREACs together using an overview paragraph*

8

OUTSIDE OF CLASS

Wake up kids. I see you're tired, you're stressed, and some of you look overwhelmed. Well, let me tell you now: you've got more to do.

Although most of you are spending every waking minute with your nose buried in your case book, studying cannot define your law school experience. If case briefs and outlines represent the totality of your law school years, you will look back on them with regret. Law school is more than just studying. You need to participate in extracurricular or co-curricular activities. Both are essential to developing professional skills and building a résumé that will land you a legal job. These are the activities that will allow you to explore your interests, develop your legal skills, cultivate important connections in the legal community, and make some genuine friends. When you look back on your law school days, the activities outside class are the ones that you will be the most proud of and you will reminisce about. More importantly, employers these days don't hire students who only spend time in class. You have to get involved and build your résumé.

Each school is different. However, the most common extra- and co-curricular activities include joining a law journal, competing in advocacy honors programs, participating in an externship or a legal clinic, working for professors, and devoting time to public and community service. Students also commonly become involved with a variety of student organizations and clubs. Most students will participate in several of these activities while in law school.

Law Journals (and Law Review)

The infamous law review. Is it all that it is made out to be? Maybe. If you want to become a law professor or a judicial clerk for a prestigious federal judge, then most likely yes. Even if your interests lie in private practice, public interest, or with government, law review is likely to open doors. Also, the experience one gets from being a law review or a law journal member can be a valuable experience. Being on law review doesn't mean that you're destined to be God's gift to the legal profession, but it can be useful to have on your résumé.

Here's an overview of what law journals are, how you become a member, and why being a law journal member can be a valuable experience.

A. What Are They?

Law journals are academic journals that publish academic articles written mostly by professors, but also by private practitioners, judges, government officials, and other legal professionals. These articles commonly attempt to explain trends in the law, explore a particularly troublesome area of the law, or describe the theoretical underpinnings of particular legal rules or court decisions. Law journals also often host symposia to explore a particular hot issue in the law, and will publish student articles, usually called "notes" or "comments."

Unlike legal journals in other countries, in the United States the vast majority of law journals are student run and edited. Most law journals will have an executive board of third-year students (or upper-division part-time students) that are responsible for the day-to-day administration. Second-year students edit the articles and ensure that the article's footnote sources are properly cited in both form and substance (a process known as cite-checking).

Different kinds of law journals exist. A school's main publication often (but not always) has "Law Review" in its title, and is commonly referred to just as the law review (e.g., the *Harvard Law Review, the Yale Law Journal*). The law review publishes articles on a wide variety of topics and is considered the school's flagship publication. Increasingly, however, schools also have a number of other specialty journals. These journals usually focus on a particular area of law, such as animal law, business or corporate law, children's rights, entertainment, the environment, human rights, labor, gender and race issues, or international law (e.g., the *Stanford Journal of International Law*, the *Columbia Journal of Gender and Law*). A small number of journals focus on regulatory, statutory, or public policy issues (e.g., the *NYU Journal of Legislation & Public Policy*). At schools with multiple law reviews, membership on the main law review is commonly considered the most prestigious.

B. How Do You Become a Member?

The criteria for becoming a member of law review or a specialty law journal vary from school to school. Usually students become members in their second year. Some law reviews will extend membership invitations based solely on first-year grades. Most school's law reviews, however, will select members based on a combination of a student's first-year grades and performance in a "write-on competition." The write-on competition often requires students to write a small paper in a discrete period of time. Some law reviews also require that students complete a citation or grammatical editing exercise. Sometimes the write-on competition occurs during the spring semester, although more commonly the competition occurs either immediately after spring final exams or in the summer.

While standards vary, success in the write-on competition requires rigorous legal analysis, clear writing, and meticulous footnoting. Students who wish to secure a place on their school's law review should consider reading a book on academic writing and law review competitions before the competition begins. Students should also know the citation rules that the law review follows (usually the Bluebook). Two good guides that provide a detailed overview are: Eugene Volokh, *Academic Legal Writing: Law Review Articles, Student Notes, Seminar Papers, and Getting on Law Review* (3d ed. 2007) and Elizabeth Fajans & Mary R. Falk, *Scholarly Writing for Law Students: Seminar Papers, Law Review Notes and Law Review Competition Papers* (3d ed. 2004).

C. Should You Try?

Being a member of a law journal is a lot of work. Yet, it has its benefits. First, it's a good experience. Students on law review spend hours doing the kind of in-depth, meticulous legal research and writing that is required of attorneys and law clerks. Law review will help you hone your ability to write effectively and to use the blue book citation manual. Law review members are also trained to pay close attention to detail. These are skills that you'll use as an attorney.

Second, law review is a credential that makes your résumé look pretty, and it will stay that way. If you're a law review member, your résumé will always say "Law Review" (not so for other activities in law school, which may disappear from your résumé once you get more practical experience). For many employers, law journal membership is seen as a proxy for good grades and strong writing skills. At the very least, employers know that law journal is a rigorous experience. Law review membership means you have likely had more practice editing, proofreading, cite-checking, and writing than other students.

On the other hand, keeping the experience in perspective is important. Working as a law journal member is time-consuming and can be stressful. Most who join consider quitting at least a few times before the semester is done. Students who have families, or who are working and attending law school part-time, may find participating in law journals particularly challenging. Although law journal membership is valuable to have on your résumé, other things in life are simply more important. Remaining married, seeing your kids grow up, and being able to afford a roof over your head certainly trump any value law journal can bring to your life.

D. Once You Are Accepted

A law journal's membership is most commonly divided into staff members and editors. On most law journals, second-year students are the staff, while third-year students serve as senior editors, including the editor-in-chief, executive editor, managing editor, senior articles editor, and senior notes or comments editor.

Your year as a law journal staff member normally will consist of three different types of work. First, as a member you will be responsible for editing, proofreading, and cite-checking articles that the law review is publishing. Usually you will do this under the supervision of a third-year student. Your main responsibility will be to ensure that the references authors rely on support the author's claims and are in proper Bluebook (or possibly ALWD) format.

Second, the journal will likely require that you write a student note or comment. Notes and comments are student-written pieces of legal scholarship that are typically shorter than the articles that faculty write and submit. A note is intended to discuss and analyze a discrete, focused legal issue or problem in depth. A comment analyzes a recent case or piece of legislation. Some law journals will also permit students to write book reviews. Usually notes and comments will be under 15,000 words long, or roughly 20–30 pages, sometimes shorter (faculty written articles vary in length but are commonly between 25,000–35,000 words). Write to impress. If you produce a well-written, interesting, original, and adequately supported note or comment, you may receive an invitation to publish the note or comment in one of the school's law journals.

Lastly, you may assist in hosting a symposium or conference. This can include planning the symposium, inviting speakers, and then working with speakers as they submit symposium articles. Working on a symposium can be a tremendous amount of work, but often will give you the opportunity to interact with faculty from other schools, judges, or practitioners with expertise in a particular area of law.

E. Board Positions and the Third Year

At the end of your second year, you may have the opportunity to apply for an executive board position. Third year law students run the administration of the law review. Executive board positions commonly consist of the editor-in-chief, an executive or managing editor, a lead articles editor, a lead notes and comments editor, and other positions. Each journal has its own rules and customs, but usually articles editors select and edit articles, notes and comments editors work with students on their written work, and managing and executive editors supervise staff in the cite-checking, proofreading, and formatting of articles.

Working on a board in your third year will keep you busy. You're responsible for ensuring that the journal runs smoothly. But a board position is a nice credential that looks good on a résumé and can be a good learning experience.

F. Maintain Perspective

One last note: failure to make the law review or law journal is not the end of your law career. Law review is a good experience, but you can become a very successful lawyer without ever participating in law review. Build your résumé in other ways. Participate in moot court. Participate in trial advocacy. Participate in negotiation or alternative dispute resolution programs. Become a research assistant for your professor. All of these activities are attractive to employers as well, and some may even provide you better training for becoming a lawyer.

Advocacy Programs

Practical skills programs, such as moot court and trial advocacy, offer hands-on experience. If you are not participating in a law journal (and even if you are), you should consider joining one of these programs.

A. What Are They?

Most schools will offer students the opportunity to participate in extra-curricular advocacy programs. The three most common are: (1) moot court (appellate advocacy); (2) mock trial (trial advocacy); and (3) negotiation or alternative dispute resolution.

In moot court, students prepare and argue a case before an appellate court. Although programs differ, students commonly write an appellate brief and then participate in a simulated appellate oral argument. Oral argument is presented to a panel of three judges, with arguments ranging from ten to thirty minutes per person. The judges are commonly law professors and members of the bench and bar. Students in a moot court honors program will likely compete as an oralist or a brief writer in regional, national, and sometimes international interscholastic competitions.

In mock trial (trial advocacy) programs, students participate in simulated trial court proceedings and focus on developing particular litigation skills. These programs can be either civil or criminal-law focused and require students to prepare a case for trial, to create a case strategy, and to use the rules of evidence in a simulated trial experience. Mock trial programs will teach you how to make an opening statement and a closing argument, conduct a direct and cross examination, and assert evidentiary objections. In a mock trial program, volunteers usually serve as witnesses, jurors, and the judge. As with moot court, trial advocacy programs often compete in regional and national competitions.

In negotiation programs, students are given practical opportunities to hone their negotiation, dispute management, and conflict resolution skills. Students are usually taught practical negotiation techniques, such as how to frame offers persuasively, how to recognize tactics by opposing counsel and debunk them, and how to use storytelling to get your client a better deal. As a practicing attorney, regardless of what practice area you end up in, you will likely use negotiation skills on a regular basis. Learning to master negotiation techniques while in law school can give provide you a huge advantage as you enter the practice of law. As with moot court and trial advocacy programs, students will often compete in simulated negotiation exercises that are held in regional and national competitions.

For some schools, students must enroll in a course as a condition for being a member of an advocacy program. For moot court, students may be required to take an advanced writing or oral advocacy course. For trial advocacy programs, students often participate in advanced evidence and trial practice courses that have simulation components to them. For negotiation programs, students may be asked to enroll in specialized or advanced negotiation courses.

B. How Do You Become a Member?

Usually schools consider advocacy programs as honor programs with strict selection criteria. Each program will have its own selection criteria, and criteria differ among schools. Most commonly, however, students are selected based on performance in an intramural competition and a student's first-year grades. Usually students must be in good academic standing to participate. Often these advocacy programs are student run with some limited faculty or alumni oversight.

As with law journals, students usually apply for a position in an advocacy program at the end of their first year of law school or over the first-year summer. Students are then members during their second year, with the opportunity to become a senior advocate or a member of an executive board during their third year.

C. Should You Try?

You should give serious thought to participating in an advocacy program. One of the main goals of any law school experience should be to develop lawyering skills that will help you enter the profession. Advocacy programs are uniquely well-suited opportunities for developing some "real-world" skills. Participation in an advocacy program will also often allow you to develop closer relationships with faculty and with alumni. It's not uncommon to hear of students being offered jobs after impressing a mock judge in a competition.

Which program is right for you? Think about your goals after law school. Moot court usually provides a significant writing experience, which is useful for most areas of practice. If you plan on being a prosecutor, a city attorney, or a public defender, then you may wish to consider trial advocacy. Trial advocacy programs provide the best training for students who plan to focus on trial work and expect to be in court a lot after graduation. If you plan on developing a transactional practice, then a negotiation program may be a good choice to help you develop a skills base to go into a business or real estate practice. Negotiation is also a necessary skill for litigators who must frequently engage in settlement discussions and mediations. No right answer exists, and all three programs develop important skills for almost any practice area.

Regardless of the program you choose, all will provide you with practical experience. You will receive valuable feedback from practicing attorneys as well as be given opportunities for networking. Employers look for participation in skills programs and, when they don't see it, they are likely to ask you why you did not participate. Having said all that, the real reason to join these programs is because they are tremendous fun. So join something! Make the most of your time in law school. You will come out of school with skills and confidence that will serve you well in the job market and in your practice. You do not later want to be asking yourself, or worse, have an employer ask you, "What the heck did you do with your time?"

Externships and Clinics

Upper-division students should actively seek out opportunities for practical training to learn the skills, habits, and techniques that are necessary to succeed in the legal profession. Students also want to make connections with the local legal community. Two other good ways of doing so are through externships or working in a legal clinic. Both of these opportunities are usually only available to second- or third-year law students.

A. An Introduction to Externships

An externship provides law students the opportunity to work in a legal office and receive unit credit towards their J.D. degree. Externships are designed to allow students to gain practical experience before entering the practice of law. Externship placements are carefully monitored by the law school to make sure the student receives a beneficial learning experience. The externship department at the law school will usually check in regularly with both the student and the supervisor at a placement to make sure the student is being assigned quality legal projects. Traditionally, externships are only available for school credit and a student's work experience could not count for unit credit if the student was also being paid. However, some schools permit a student to receive school credit even if the student is working in a paid position.

The types of externships and their structure can vary. Externship placements may be with judges, in-house legal departments, public interest organizations, or federal, state, and local government offices. In some circumstances externships are offered with private law firms and other for-profit organizations. Externships usually are a semester long or in the summer and, in many schools, students can enroll in part-time or full-time externships. Occasionally, students can enroll in a full-time externship abroad. Demand for, and participation in, externships have increased significantly in recent years in schools across the country.

Students should seek out externships opportunities for a number of reasons. First, externships provide students with a unique opportunity to be immersed in hands-on, practical legal training and experiential learning. Second, externships provide students an opportunity to build connections in the legal community and gain a better understanding of real-life law practice. Externships allow students to make connections that could lead to full-time employment. For highly-competitive public interest jobs, an externship may almost be a prerequisite for a job after graduation. Increasingly, an externship is considered a good leg up to getting any job in a tough legal market. Externships can be a great résumé builder and an opportunity to develop real-world legal skills.

B. An Introduction to Clinics

Legal clinics are law school programs that provide hands-on legal experience to students under close supervision. The clinic usually occupies a physical space that is either in the law school or near to it. A full-time clinical faculty member will usually direct and be responsible for overseeing and supervising the student members, and is often supported by some administrative staff (paralegals, social workers, secretaries, etc.). Clinics typically do public service and community-based work, providing free legal services to the indigent and underserved populations. The area of specialization for clinics varies dramatically. Some common clinic focuses include animal law, bankruptcy, children's rights, community law, criminal defense, domestic violence, elder law, employment and wage claims, environmental law, family, human rights, immigration, landlord/tenant, mediation, small business, street law, and tax.

The work a student can expect in a clinical experience also varies depending on the clinic's focus. Students will typically provide assistance with legal research, writing memorandum, and drafting legal documents, as well as client-intake and meeting and interviewing clients or witnesses. In many jurisdictions, courts have "student practice" rules that allow clinic students to be certified and then appear and argue in court or before an administrative law judge. Often a classroom component (such as a clinic seminar or clinic course) will provide students with the necessary foundation and background in the relevant law.

Clinical experiences are usually offered during the fall or spring semester of the second and third year. Students should make it a priority to enroll in a clinic prior to graduation as not only a way to do community service, but as a way to develop practical lawyering skills that will be useful upon graduation. Legal clinical experience is valued by employers and looks great on a résumé. Clinics are known to be selective in the students they choose, and participation allows chosen students to develop relationships with mentors in an intimate environment. That intimate environment with top-notch attorneys has the potential to open doors for students.

Other Opportunities

After the first year, students have more time to dedicate to activities outside the classroom. Students should look into opportunities that interest them, without spreading themselves too thin. Here is an overview of what some of those opportunities are:

A. Teaching and Research Assistant Positions

Yes, the opportunity you have all been waiting for with bated breath... the chance to work for your professors. Most professors will hire upper-division students either to assist with a course (i.e., as a teaching assistant) or with research on an article or book project that the professor is working on (i.e., as a research assistant).

This is something you should not pass up. After all, professors are often experts in their field and will likely provide you with a golden opportunity to work on a new and upcoming legal issue. This can be very helpful in assisting you in your job search. Imagine this: you work for a professor researching the newest intellectual property issue; you then go and interview with an intellectual property firm and are able to discuss this up-to-date issue with the practicing attorneys.

You will also develop a professional relationship with your professor. Working for a professor gives you a once-in-a-lifetime opportunity to get the personal attention of your professor. You will have a personal guide as to how you are advancing in your ability to perform research and legal analysis. Perhaps most importantly — unlike externships, clinics, law journals or advocacy programs — you will get paid. Most professors are able to pay students to serve as teaching and research assistants through federal work study or other faculty funds.

B. Student Organizations

Most law schools have literally dozens and dozens of student organizations and groups that students can participate in. These organizations are based on social, political, service and professional interests and will hold almost daily events. Student organizations provide a good way for students to meet and get to know other students with similar backgrounds, interests or goals.

Schools will often have 20–40 different student organizations and their focus will be varied. Some groups focus on substantive areas of the law (e.g., the Business Law Association, the Criminal Law Society, the Environmental Law Society, International Law Society, Intellectual Property Law Society, etc.), while others are politically or religiously focused (e.g., the Federalist Society, the Christian Legal Society, the Muslim Law Students Association, the Democratic or Republican Student Associations, etc.), and others are based on social or ethnic groups (e.g., the Black Law

Students Association, the Native American Law Students Association, the Older Wiser Law Students Association, OUTlaws, the Latino Law Students Association, the Women's Law Association, etc.). Some are purely social in nature and sponsor intramural sports (e.g., the Golf Association or the Law and Wine Society). Some schools will have a student-run newspaper or a Law Revue — an annual comedy and musical production — that students can be involved with.

Should you participate in a student organization? During your undergraduate study, you were likely a member of the pre-law society in the hopes it would build your résumé and help you get into law school. In reality, participation in such groups probably had little to do with your acceptance into any law school. The same holds true now that you are in law school. Your participation in a student group is unlikely to directly land you the job of your dreams. You should join a student group because you have a genuine interest in that group and because you will meet others with similar interests. You can get to know your classmates and have a forum for socializing. These friends will be useful contacts in your future practice of law. Moreover, they will be your friends, possibly for a lifetime.

C. Faculty/Student and SBA Committees

In addition to student organizations, many schools will permit students to sit on faculty/student committees. Some committees that are common include student life committee, student enhancement committee, admissions committee, curriculum committee, building committee, and library committee. Some schools will allow students to be involved in faculty appointments and alumni development.

Students also have the opportunity at many schools to participate in the Student Bar Association (or SBA). The duties, structure, and size of the SBA various among law schools. But for most schools, the SBA is the official student governing body. Through its activities, the SBA advocates student concerns, coordinates student activities and organizations, and is usually charged with appropriating funds for student activities. The SBA Board will usually consist of student representatives from each class (and from different programs, if available at your school). The SBA will have an executive board that will consist usually of a president, vice president, secretary, and treasurer. Students have a number of opportunities to become involved with the SBA.

D. Public Service and Volunteering

Law school will be a hectic time for you and you will probably feel as if you could not possibly squeeze in any other activities or commitments. Despite that, students should not graduate without some public service or pro bono legal experience. Volunteering for non-profit legal, governmental, or community organizations is a valuable opportunity to gain experience and provides students a good opportunity to develop connections in the legal community. Pro bono legal services are done under the supervision of a practicing lawyer, and students may not receive compensation — either pay or academic credit — for doing pro bono work. Public service work is rewarding, helps students develop lawyering skills, teaches students how to work with clients, allows students to gain exposure to various substantive areas of the law, and enhances a résumé. Most importantly, public service work serves those in your community who have limited access to legal representation.

Most schools have a number of options for students who wish to gain experience through public service. Many schools have extensive public service or pro bono programs, or even public interest law centers, dedicated offices, or institutes. Some schools require that students complete a minimum amount of mandatory pro bono (without pay or unit credit) public service before graduating. Only a very small number of schools have no organized public service program.

Schools often provide incentives for students to devote time to public service. Many schools will award scholarships or fellowships for students who wish to assist indigent clients, under-represented groups, and non-profit organizations. Part-time and full-time opportunities usually will exist both in the school year and in the summer. Some schools will also fund a limited number of post-graduate public service fellowships. And some schools provide loan-forgiveness for students who intend to enter a public interest law career.

How much public service work should you do? If your goal is to work with a nonprofit or public interest organization after graduation, then quite a bit. These jobs are highly competitive. A career in public interest law typically requires a demonstrated commitment to public interest work. Public interest employers generally want to know that you have a genuine commitment to serving others. Even if you hope to work in the private for-profit sector or in government, you should consider doing a considerable amount of public service work while in law school (maybe 25–75 hours each year). Doing public service activities may be one of the best ways to gain hands-on practical training in law school and is generally valued by employers. Many private law firms are involved in supervising pro bono work, and volunteering can be one of the best ways to meet these attorneys and make connections in the legal community.

Okay, that about covers it. Get involved. I'll see you next class.

Checklist Reminders

Key Points

- ❑ *Do something, anything — just get involved!*
- ❑ *Why? Need to develop practical lawyering skills — improve legal research, writing, analysis, interviewing, counseling, oral advocacy, client interaction, etc.*
- ❑ *Getting involved may be key to getting a job.*

Activities to Consider

- ❑ *Law review or law journal*
- ❑ *Externships*
- ❑ *Clinical work*
- ❑ *Appellate advocacy / moot court*
- ❑ *Trial advocacy / mock trial*
- ❑ *Negotiation or alternative dispute resolution programs*
- ❑ *Research assistant*
- ❑ *Teaching assistant*
- ❑ *Student bar association*
- ❑ *Student organizations and clubs*
- ❑ *Volunteer, public service, and community organizations*
- ❑ *Faculty-student committee*
- ❑ *The law revue (singing and dancing in law school?) or the student newspaper*

9

BEYOND LAW SCHOOL

The actual practice of law may seem like the horizon to you: you can see it clearly, but it's distant and unapproachable. As far away as it seems now, your plans for the future should be ever in your thoughts. Your time in law school cannot be spent focused solely on class; you must also seize opportunities to advance your career goals.

Preparing for Your Career

Keep the end goal in mind. Graduation is not the end zone; you do not spike the ball for the touchdown. You should look beyond graduation day with you in a cap and gown, standing next to proud smiling relatives. For most of you, the object of your legal education is to become a practicing attorney. Ultimately, you must find someone who is willing to employ you. A job search in the legal profession, like other job markets, is an exercise in selling yourself. So look for opportunities throughout law school to make yourself more marketable. You need to start thinking about building a résumé and getting practical legal experience after your first year of law school.

Your first year will be an exercise in keeping your head above water. Your focus should be primarily on school and how to succeed in class. However, there are a few things you can do to get a step ahead during your first year (cultivating relationships with your professors, for example). Once you have closed the book on the last of your first-year exams, take a deep breath and head full force into planning your sales pitch.

A. Cultivate Relationships

The first step in your marketing campaign is to get some heavy hitters to go to bat for you. You need someone to speak convincingly on your behalf and your professors need to be able to say more than just "Dante did well in my class, he writes excellent case briefs." When asking a professor for a reference or letter of recommendation, it helps if they can actually pick you out of a crowd.

Recall the words of wisdom on the importance of developing relationships with your professors. Consider the following scenario, a student walks into his professor's office and says "Professor, could you please write me a letter of recommendation? Oh and let me introduce myself, I am Amanda Farias." Both the response and any letter I might write will be lacking in the enthusiasm required to dazzle potential employers.

How can you make contact with your professors? Here are several different ways you can begin building those relationships that will lead to references and letters of recommendation.

Ask Questions: Don't have a question? Make one up, if not about the material, about how the material applies to a particular situation (the question does not have to be brilliant, just not idiotic). If appropriate, ask the professor questions on topics outside of class or about their experiences in the practice of law and share your goals with them. Don't do this once; commit yourself to having a conversation with a professor several times in a semester. Once or twice a month is ideal.

Find a Mentor: By the end of your first year you will inevitably have begun thinking about what kind of law you want to practice. Sit down with professors with expertise in areas of interest. From speaking with them, you will be able to more accurately define your career goals and get valuable employment advice. Ultimately you will gain a mentor and a reference. You should also consider trying to get connected with alumni, who also may be wonderful mentors too.

Take Advantage of Academic Writing Opportunities: In the beginning of your second year, you will likely embark on a fabulous journey into the world of academic writing. Perhaps you will begin this journey through your position on law review. Others will have the opportunity by taking an upper division seminar class. Who best to steer you through the perils and frustrations of publishing an article than those who have gone before you. Many, if not all, of your professors are published academics. Identify a professor, or two or three, who have some expertise on the subject of your article. Build a team of coaches who look at your topic from many different angles and consult with them regularly.

Become a Research or Teaching Assistant: A research assistant or teaching assistant position will allow you to develop a close working relationship with a professor. If you do a good job, you may find someone who can tell future employers about your brilliant analytical mind and the quality of your research and writing skills.

B. Get Practical Experience

Three years from now you will be ready to begin your job search. As you assess your résumé you'll be thinking to yourself, hmmm, graduated from law school... check; passed the bar exam... check; top of the class, on law review, great references... check, check, check. Brilliant, right? Wrong. The idiosyncrasies of a legal job search suddenly become apparent. As strange as it might sound, legal employers expect you have some actual legal experience before you graduate from law school. Fortunately, opportunities are abound in law school for you to get the kind of practical experience employers will expect.

You should not graduate without taking advantage of some of the opportunities available to you. After you finish your first year, it's time to dive in to participate in externships, clinics, summer internships, research and teaching assistant positions, advocacy programs, and student organizations. Make an effort to add several of these experiences to your résumé.

C. Take Advanced Writing/Skills Courses

As a lawyer, you will write constantly and as a new lawyer it is your writing ability that will make you most valuable to the partners in your firm. As writing ability is one of the most prized skills that legal employers value, any honors you receive in a legal writing course should be included on your résumé. Then be sure to fit an advanced skills course into your schedule before you graduate. Most law schools offer advanced legal research and writing, most also offer appellate advocacy and pretrial practice courses. These kinds of courses are essential preparations for your ensuing legal career.

D. Meet with the Careers Office

Chances are there is a door you walk by every day on your way to class with a sign "Career Service Office" (or something similar). You've been so busy briefing, outline, studying, panicking and so on that it has never occurred to you that there might be very smart people behind that door who know exactly how to get you a job. Wouldn't it be great to have someone who has been in the business for years tell you what to emphasize on your résumé to get an employer's attention, and what common mistakes will send your résumé to the trash pile on an employer's desk? It's time to take that leap, cross that threshold, and get some expert help. You may not realize all the valuable help and advice waiting for you in this office:

- Résumé and cover letter samples
- Tips on how to design and improve your résumé
- Help in planning your career goals
- Help in applying for summer internships
- Access to online databases with nationwide job postings
- On-campus interviewing opportunities
- Practice interview questions
- Mock interview practice
- Marketing materials sent to out-of-state firms
- Networking opportunities
- Career days and job fairs

The list goes on and on. The career services office is your ambassador to employment and you must use their expertise. You merely need to want a job badly enough to walk through the door. They will meet you more than halfway.

E. Jump at Networking Opportunities

There it is, the dreaded word: Networking. You have likely wondered what networking really means and how exactly you are supposed to engage in this well-known professional ritual. Let's start with what networking is not. Networking does not mean approaching those you do not know (or have just met) and asking them for a job. It is, simply put, you getting to know other professionals in the legal community. It is a way to build connections that may be helpful to you in the future.

How do you "network"? When you attend an event where other professionals are present, make an attempt to meet attorneys in the community and get to know them. Do not regale them with your many qualifications and in no way expect that your conversations will lead to a job (not at first, at least). This is not an interview, it is a conversation. Be your normal, witty, charming self (unless your normal self is not so charming and witty, in which case pretend this is an interview—in other words, be professional). Enjoy the company of people who share similar interests and who will almost certainly have valuable and insightful thoughts to offer on the practice of law.

I can hear you asking, "But doesn't networking mean I rub elbows with influential people, and they adore me on the spot for my wit and gumption and give me the corner office?" The popular perception is misleading. It is true that those whom fortune favors may find that a networking opportunity places a job right in their lap. A former student of mine had such an experience. This enterprising student wanted to attend a golf tournament knowing several attorneys in the community were participating. Unfortunately, the cost of the tournament was too steep for a first-year law student. Not one to give up easily, the student called up those in charge and arranged to participate for free given his status as a starving law student. At the tournament, he met three attorneys who ultimately offered him a summer clerkship position.

This is the exception, not the rule. Your real hope is that any contacts you make may turn into an opportunity at some point in the future and any effort you make to get to know other professionals in your field will likely pay off in some form. Perhaps you will end up applying at the attorney's firm in the future. Perhaps you will face the attorney as opposing counsel at some point and your relationship will help you reach a favorable settlement. At a minimum, you will likely learn what a law career is like in a certain field and this can help you shape your career goals. You may learn about a field of law you had never thought of before and broaden your career opportunities.

How can you find these all-important, much talked-of networking opportunities? Start with events put on by your law school. Your school likely has alumni events where practicing attorneys come back to meet current law students. Really anytime there is an on-campus event which includes practicing attorneys you should make an effort to attend and meet new people. Then look for opportunities outside law school. Your local bar association is a good starting place as they often sponsor events where you are sure to meet other professionals. Finally, think beyond the obvious — follow the example of my student who scored a free ticket to a golf tournament with nothing but initiative.

One last point, just so there is no confusion: networking is not the only path to gainful employment. Most of you will find a job the traditional way, by sending in a résumé and interviewing. It is a logical certainty, however, that the more people you know in the legal community, the more likely one of those connections will pan out and assist you in some way in the future.

F. Consider All of Your Options

Some of you came to law school with a specific career plan in mind. You might know you want to practice criminal defense or bankruptcy when you graduate. Most of you have no idea in what area of the law you would like to practice. In making your decision, pay attention to all opportunities available to you. Consider what else is available and evaluate which career best fits your life goals. Maybe you have dreamed of that big firm job and the large salary that accompanies it. Others may have decided to sacrifice salary a little in exchange for a better work-life balance. Either way, most of you probably anticipate being employed by some type of law firm, big or small. In reality there are many options available to you outside of a law firm.

Government Positions: If you haven't already done so, consider practicing as a government attorney. Government positions can be criminal, such as the district attorney's office or public defender's office, or civil, such as the city attorney's office. Opportunities exist at the local (municipal), regional (county), state, and federal level. Don't limit yourself to looking just at your state or local government; consider the abundance of federal jobs available as well. After all, a steady salary, full benefits, great pension, and a sense of civic duty make for a great career!

Non-Profit Organizations: Pursue a career in public interest and give back to those in need. If you have not already been in contact with your public interest law society on campus (or public interest center), look them up and ask how you can become involved. Working in the area of public interest is extremely rewarding as you generally help underprivileged or underserved clients in need of an attorney. The Human Rights Project, for example, works to gain asylum for immigrants subject to persecution in their home countries. Legal Aid attorneys generally provide legal services to low-income clients facing eviction, foreclosure, deportation, or who are victims of domestic violence. These are just two of many public interest groups working for those who would normally never be able to afford legal assistance. Although many law students become involved in some type of public interest during law school, far fewer actually pursue a career in that area after graduation. Consider doing so. You may not get paid the big bucks, but you will make a salary you can be proud of and you will add meaning to your life and career.

Judicial Clerkships: A judicial clerkship is an opportunity to work in a judge's chambers for usually one or two years immediately following graduation. Judicial clerkships are often fiercely competitive, but if you can land one it will give you an opportunity to work directly with a judge. You will see how a trial works from behind the scenes and have a say in the outcome of the cases you work on. In essence, a judicial clerkship allows you to assist in making law. The salary of a judicial clerk may not be comparable to a big-firm salary, but a clerkship only lasts one to two years and it looks great on your résumé — making you more marketable when your clerkship is over. Some students only focus on federal district or appellate clerkships. Don't limit yourself. A judicial clerkship with a state court can be great experience.

Legal Fellowships: Through a legal fellowship you will learn a specific area of law by practicing for an organization with a particular legal philosophy. The philosophies are diverse: the Christian Legal Fellowship, for instance, offers fellowships with a Christian world view while the ACLU offers fellowships based in a particular political perspective. Fellowships allow you to assume significant responsibility right out of law school and you are usually assigned cutting-edge cases. A fellowship usually lasts for one to two years and is a great segue to a future career in a specialized area of law. Your career services office will have information about the various legal fellowships available to you.

Solo Practitioner: Maybe you are a do-it-on-your-own type of person. Many attorneys eventually decide to fly solo and open up their own office.

This may prove difficult immediately upon graduation as you will have little practical experience and no established clientele. Although challenging, if a solo career is what you have your heart set on, it is not impossible. This is one area where networking will be essential. If you have met sufficient contacts in the legal community, you can get referrals from your new friends. Get as much practical experience in law school as possible. Participate in as many externships as possible. Try a clinic. Take practical skills courses. Keep in mind that experience will come with time and so will the clients. A number of good books, websites, and blogs are dedicated to explaining how to start a solo practice. Those resources are good places to start.

In choosing among these (and other) options, try to focus on more than prestige and money. Think about which career path works best for your professional ambitions and other life goals. Any new graduate has some grunt work to do and must "pay their dues" — you won't be arguing that seminal U.S. Supreme Court case the day after your graduate. Still, thinking about your long-term goals are important. Are you one who would like to have children and spend time with them? Do you like to travel? Are you willing to move to another city if your employer requires it? Evaluate what your existing commitments are and whether a particular job will allow you to meet them. Evaluate any job offer based on whether it will allow you to be fulfilled in all aspects of your life. Don't be afraid to pursue an entirely different direction than the one in which you may have started out.

Letters of Recommendation

Once you have developed that prized professional relationship with your professor, you will need to ask for the reference or letter of recommendation. When asking for a reference, you must remain personal and professional. Here are some specific tips to keep in mind.

A. Make Good Choices

For almost all recommendation letters you must make good choices on who you ask. Getting an "A" or "A+" in a course is not enough. You must have a recommender who is able to provide thoughtful insights into your intellectual abilities, and usually your writing, research, and analytical skills. The best letters often are able to address your ability to critically analyze complete facts and legal doctrines, as well as your ability to articulate cogent and effective legal arguments. Better yet, you want a recommendation letter that comments on your personal traits — these kinds of letters often sound more genuine and persuasive. You only want recommendation letters from professors who can provide a strong recommendation. If you sense reluctance on the part of the professor, ask someone else.

B. Approach Recommenders Directly

Personal conversations are much better than impersonal emails when asking for a recommendation letter. Use emails only for quick questions with short answers. They do not count towards your goal of building a relationship with your professor. Be professional in all your communications with your professors, email and in person. You are building your professional reputation from your first day in law school. Your professionalism, or lack thereof, is something that your professors will certainly comment on in any letter of recommendation and something that every employer will consider.

C. Ask, Don't Presume

Make sure when you ask for a reference or letter of recommendation, you do just that — ASK! Never presume. Don't notify your professor that you have put him/her down as a reference. Ask if the professor is willing to serve as a reference Ask in person. Asking for a reference or letter of recommendation in person is a way to re-connect with your professor and keep the relationship that you have been working on fresh in their minds. It is also much more personal and professional to see your professor and ask for the courtesy in person.

D. Give Plenty of Notice

Professors are busy. When asking for a letter of recommendation, give your professors plenty of advance notice to write the letter. Give me at least two weeks' notice (if not more), whenever possible. Providing plenty of notice increases not only the chance that they will write the letter, but also the chance the letter will be one of quality.

E. Make It Easy for the Recommender

Make things easy for the recommender to send the letter. Be sure to provide the address or website where the letter must be sent, and any forms that need to be included with the letter. If there are forms that need to be completed, complete the basic information that needs to be filled out about you and the recommender's contact information. Most importantly, be sure to provide the deadline for the letter.

F. Provide Detailed Information

Don't presume your professors know you as well as you do. Even if your recommender knows you well, they may not remember every bit of your life story that could be helpful in writing a letter. Ask your professors if they would like you to send them: (1) your résumé; (2) your unofficial transcript; (3) your personal statement (if one is required for the application); or (4) a copy of your best work for the professor or a summary of your other accomplishments. Remind your professor of any specific details that might be helpful in writing the letter (e.g., you scored the top grade in the class, you received an award for your performance, etc.). This will give the writer a better opportunity to comment thoroughly on your abilities and qualifications.

Be sure to tell your recommenders all the places you are applying, and try not to blindside them with seriatim requests for additional letters. Providing a full list of the programs and places you are applying at once is much easier than having to send out many letters in small batches.

G. Remember to Follow Up

Let your recommenders know what happens. Also, sometimes letters get lost or professors forget to write them. Double-check that your letter arrived. Finally, be sure to thank the recommender with a short thank you card or note.

The Summer Placement

A few tips for those of you who have landed a summer job or internship with a law firm.

A. Act Professionally

Remember, you are here to make an impression. Perhaps you are hoping for a full time job. At a minimum, you will need your employer to serve as a reference. To make the right impression, you need to display professional behavior throughout the entire experience.

Show up on time — every day and for everything. If you are asked to be at the office at 8:00 a.m., your supervising attorney will expect to see you there at 8:00 a.m. Not 8:05. Not 8:15. In fact, your supervising attorney will likely walk by your office at 8:00 a.m. just to see if you are there. Shock them — show up at 7:45! Traffic and your alarm not going off are not good excuses for being late. If a meeting begins at 11:00 a.m., be sure to be there before it starts. You can't afford to be late.

Be genuinely friendly and nice to everyone in the firm. You need to be respectful to not just the partners or associates at the firm, but the secretaries, paralegals, law librarians, security guards, and other staff. The staff will be asked their opinion of you by the hiring partners so make sure they like you. Be respectful to other summer clerks as well. They may turn out to be your colleagues in the future.

A related point: be modest. No matter how smart you think you are, you know almost nothing about practicing law. So, for the sake of your own career, don't pretend that you do. Firms don't like summer clerks/interns who are pretentious, and they won't offer them jobs after graduation.

B. Dress Professionally

Be sure to dress as others do in the office and err on the side of being conservative (okay, boring) in how you dress. Most of the time for most law offices, you should wear a dark suit, a white shirt or blouse, and, if a man, a conservative tie. This is not the time for lime green shirts, Technicolor-swirl ties, and light-colored, five-button blazers found only on fashion runways. If there's a casual Friday, don't be too casual. Again, be conservative. Don't wear anything too flashy or sexy.

C. Submit Assignments on Time

Turn all assignments in on time. If you are given a deadline and you will not be able to make it, tell your supervising attorney at the time you are given the assignment. Yes, it is okay to tell a supervising attorney that you have too many deadlines to complete their project on time. That is, if you really do have that much work. Telling your supervising attorney you cannot meet a deadline because of a baseball game or a baby shower will not bode well. If you discover after you receive an assignment that you will not be able to finish the project in time, tell your supervising attorney at the moment you realize that you cannot make the deadline — never wait until the deadline to let them know it is not finished, and never let the deadline pass without turning in the assignment or speaking with your supervisor.

D. Always Bring a Pen and Paper

Show up to meetings with a pen and a legal pad or notebook. Anytime an attorney asks you to come to their office or attend a meeting, you will likely need to take notes. You will not be able to remember everything your supervising attorney tells you and you appear unprofessional to presume that you can. So have a stack of notebooks ready and always grab one on your way in to talk to an attorney.

E. Ask Appropriate Questions

As law students, you are not expected to know everything. Your employer will know this is your first legal experience and you are just getting your feet wet. Although they will not expect you to know everything, they will expect you to ask questions when you are unclear on the assignment or task. You must ensure that you understand every assignment you are given.

Ask questions to clarify exactly what end product your supervisor is expecting. Does she want oral feedback on your research? Does he want a written product, such as an office memorandum? Does your supervisor want you to actually draft a brief or motion? Ask question to clarify how much time you should spend on a project. Perhaps your supervisor thinks the project can be done in 10 hours. You don't want to come back to your supervisor with the project after having billed 20 hours.

Ask questions as you are completing and after you have completed the project. You should never guess what to do. If you do not know an answer, simply take the time to walk down to the attorney's office, tell them what you have, and ask your question. Bring what you have completed with you. At some point, you also want to ask for feedback. Only with feedback will you be able to improve, and most supervisors want to see new attorneys excel and succeed.

Although asking questions is critical, you must first attempt to find the answer to the question on your own. When you go to a supervising attorney with a question, start by telling the attorney what efforts you have made to find the answer. One excellent source for answers are practice guides. Every jurisdiction has "how-to" practice guides to guide attorneys on legal questions. In Texas, try the magical Dorsaneo's Texas Litigation Guide. In California, Witkin's California Materials is a great resource. Often, there are several practice guides in a jurisdiction. Get to know your favorite and use it as a source to help you when you are not sure of your next steps. Remember, these are just practice guides, they are not the law. Don't cite to them as authority for a memorandum or brief to the court.

F. Work Hard

Your clerkship/internship is your opportunity to impress practicing attorneys and to learn. There is a chance that your summer job will lead to an offer of full time employment. Some summer clerkships give the appearance that you are there merely to be catered to and enjoy yourself. If you are clerking for a large firm with a "summer program," you will likely be taken to the spa, golfing, sports games, etc. Don't let these fun activities mislead you. You are there to work and make a good impression. Even if it appears the firm does not expect you to work hard, work hard. Work very hard. They are watching to see who will step up to the plate.

When I say work hard, however, you want to keep standard hours. If most associates are arriving at 8:30 am and leaving at 6:30 pm, you should too. You don't want to be eccentric. Don't keep strange hours (like beginning at 11 am and working until midnight). The people you work with will not be impressed and will start wondering why you are taking so much longer than others getting your work finished.

G. Proofread. Proofread. Proofread.

Did I say that enough times? I can't overemphasize how important it is. Good attorneys are meticulous, perhaps even to a fault. Your work product means little if it is smothered with spelling mistakes, grammar errors, and other symptoms of poor writing (e.g., excessive use of passive voice, nominalizations, long-winded sentences etc.). Actually, any kind of typo can undermine your credibility. You want to turn in work product — even when the partner asks for a draft — that is professionally formatted, has no typos or grammatical errors, and is written in a clear, easy-to-read writing style. Equally unhelpful is a memo or brief that relies on bad law. Make sure to Shepardize all your cases and cite-check carefully. Appearance is more than half the game.

A related point. Quality of work is usually always more important than quantity. If it takes you a month to write a four-page memo, you're in trouble, but summer clerks are almost always evaluated on the quality of the work they submit and not the sheer amount of work completed. Make each project count.

H. Go to Firm Functions

As mentioned, your summer employer may have special functions for the summer clerks or interns: dinners or wine tastings, a baseball game, whitewater rafting trips, a round of golf, or a spa day. I know what you are thinking — no one will have to twist your arms to get you there! When you start your summer clerkship and realize your firm has an event every evening, sheer exhaustion may tempt you to skip the ones that are less interesting you. Don't. Your employer will spend the summer evaluating not just your work product, but how well you fit into the firm, not to mention your commitment and stamina. They expect you to go to all the functions unless you have a darn good reason to miss (completing a work assignment on time is a good reason). Show up, smile, and act like you are having the time of your life even if you are tired of spending every evening with the same people you see all day at work. Going to firm events shows an interest in the firm.

Don't be fooled, the firm functions and events are part of your summer-long interview for this job. Treat the events like interviews. No matter how casual the event — and even if partners and associates are acting outrageously — you are under constant evaluation. Don't blow it. For many employers, social events are intended to see how you interact with other people. This doesn't mean you shouldn't enjoy yourself. However, don't let your guard down too much. This is not the time to be revealing past indiscretions or any other personal thing about you that may reflect badly. You must continue to act professionally.

Some obvious points, but perhaps worth emphasizing. If you drink, drink in moderation (moderation at most firms is one or possibly two drinks in an evening). Never get buzzed at a firm event. Also, don't try to date partners, associates, or summer associates. I'm not going into more detail. It's a bad idea, and hopefully you understand why. A last obvious point — never tell crude or vulgar jokes.

I. Take Advantage of Firm Training

Many private law firms will offer summer clerks some training workshops. It may be a deposition workshop, or a writing workshop, or a session on client development. Take advantage of any training programs or workshops offered. They usually provide you important insight into what the firm expects of you, and also provide you with an opportunity to get to know (and possibly impress) more firm associates and partners. Failing to attend these training workshops may suggest that you're not sufficiently interested in the firm.

After Graduation

The first year of practice may be overwhelming regardless of which career path you choose. You will be learning a whole new area of law or trying to quickly absorb the intricacies and nuances of one you thought you had learned in law school. Unlike in law school, you now have real clients who depend upon your competence. Here are some important things to keep in mind as you make this transition and begin your career.

A. Build a Professional Reputation

Judges talk. Lawyers talk. They especially love to talk about other attorneys. Sometimes they talk about new attorneys who have impressed them. Usually they spend their time talking about the humorous and inappropriate behavior displayed by unprofessional attorneys. Anytime you think it is not important to be on time, or to dress professionally, or to make strong arguments in support of your position, think about the judges and senior attorneys sitting around at lunch laughing at you. Think about how quickly your actions will spread throughout the legal community and affect your career.

The manner in which you conduct yourself in the courtroom or in a negotiation will soon be known to all. Within your first year of practice (even within the first few months) you will have established a reputation for what type of lawyer you are. Think now about what you want that reputation to be. Will you be a professional who behaves respectfully to judges, opposing attorneys, and court personnel? Will you be known as a thoughtful, hardworking attorney who takes the time to develop strong

arguments supported by law? Will you be known as intellectually honest? Will judges know you as someone whose written briefs are designed
to persuade but not mislead and which never leave out important case
law that supports the other side? Will you be known as someone who
manages their time well in order to get all assignments done on time and
not at the last minute? Perhaps most importantly, are you someone who
practices law with integrity and unimpeachable ethics or do you practice
using shady tactics, skirting the ethics laws to the point of being just shy
of breaking them?

How you dress and speak, the quality of your work product, and how
you treat others is critical to your success as an attorney. This is not to say
that you can never make a mistake. You will make mistakes. Count on it.
Your character is revealed by how you deal with the mistake. New lawyers
tend to try to hide the mistake and hope it goes away. This can only end
badly for your client and your career. Good attorneys go immediately to
their supervisor and get help fixing the mistake. Good lawyers never make
the same mistake again.

B. Join Local Bar Associations

In most states a large number of local bar associations exist. Some are
organized geographically (e.g., the Beverly Hills Bar Association, Santa
Monica Bar Association, and the Glendale Bar Association), others are
organized by personal characteristics (e.g., the Black Women Lawyer's
Bar Association, LGBTQ+ Bar Association, and the Iranian-American
Bar Association), and some are organized by practice area (e.g., the Los
Angeles Intellectual Property Law Association, the Labor & Employment
Law Section of the Los Angeles County Bar Association, and the Individual Rights Section of the Los Angeles County Bar Association). Local
and specialty bar associations are in some ways social clubs where you
can network, meet new friends, and learn about the substantive area of
law and your business. Whether you are a sole practitioner, a partner in a
small firm, or are working for a giant mega-firm, networking is important
to build your law practice and increase your visibility in the profession.
Joining a bar association is a good way to do that. Most bar associations
will have mixers and continuing legal education events throughout the
year.

C. Keep in Contact

Once you become a practicing lawyer, don't close the book on law school. It is imperative that you maintain your law school relationships after law school as they will be valuable to you in the future.

Let's start with your law school friends. Imagine this. You are working at a mid-sized firm following graduation and things seem to be going well. Then the senior partner in the firm walks in your office and starts talking to you about partnership and the requirement that you start bringing in clients. Where are you going to find the clients? Well, if you have kept in touch with everyone in law school, you will have a source of attorneys who can refer clients to you that their firm is not able to serve. Or, imagine your senior partner came to tell you the firm is merging and you may need to find a new job. Wouldn't it be nice if you kept in touch with those who may have an opening at their firm?

Now let's talk about those important law school professors. Perhaps you are working as a judicial clerk and your clerkship ends. You now need a new job and that job requires references. Wouldn't you like to know you have kept in touch with your professors so you can easily call them up and ask them to be a reference? The longer it has been since you spoke to that professor, the more difficult it will be to ask them to be a reference. So keep in touch over the years in one fashion or another.

One way to keep in touch is to go back to your law school and volunteer. Most law schools need judges for moot court/negotiation competitions or have alumni events where you can reconnect with your professors and classmates. As an alum, you should go back and help your school. It just happens that this is also a good way to maintain relationships that will be rewarding to you and helpful to you on a professional level.

D. Remain Flexible in Your Career

Hopefully when you graduate you will have a job lined up and you will love it. Unfortunately, the majority of you will not yet have found your dream job. Perhaps you even have a job lined up and you think it is the dream job. You may discover your boss is a nightmare or that you can't possibly practice that type of law for the rest of your life. No worries. Things change. Remain flexible. Keep your eye out. You are never stuck in a job you don't enjoy. Find the job that makes you want to get up in the morning and go to work. Find the job that makes you proud to be a lawyer, and never give up looking for it until it is yours.

——————————————

That's all for today. I'm done.

Checklist Reminders

The Basics

- ❑ *Cultivate relationships with professors while at law school (at some point will need recommendation letters)*
- ❑ *Get as much practical hands-on experience as possible (think externships, clinics, summer jobs)*
- ❑ *Make alumni connections and network*
- ❑ *Take advanced writing courses in second and third years (the more the better)*
- ❑ *Enroll in advanced skill and capstone courses*
- ❑ *Take advantage of the Career Services Office and plan a job-search strategy*

Letters of Recommendation

- ❑ *Ask only people (professors) I know well*
- ❑ *Ask in person for a letter of recommendation (not by email or phone)*
- ❑ *Ask before using someone as a reference*
- ❑ *Give plenty of notice for professors to write a letter of recommendation (2 weeks minimum)*
- ❑ *Provide detailed information about self (résumé, transcript, copy of best work, etc.)*
- ❑ *Follow up*
- ❑ *Send thank you notes to recommenders*

The Summer Job

- ❑ *Act professionally and be friendly to everyone*
- ❑ *Dress conservatively and professionally*
- ❑ *Always bring pen and paper when meeting with supervisors*

❑ Be clear as to expectations and what supervisor/client wants before beginning project

❑ Always submit assignments on time

❑ Be extra-meticulous with all written work product (proofread to ensure no typos or errors) — there's no such thing as a draft!

❑ Actively seek out feedback

❑ Go to firm functions and get to know supervisors, partners, and other attorneys

❑ Treat all events as interviews

❑ Work hard — you've got one chance!

After Graduation

❑ Reputation is everything!

❑ Join local bar and community organizations

❑ Continue to network with law school alumni (get a mentor!)

❑ Stay in contact with classmates

❑ Stay in contact with your school

❑ Keep your eye out for opportunities

10

THE BAR EXAM

Well, let me say it. I'm stunned. You made it. Walked across that stage and made all of your relatives proud. You have one last hurdle — to pass the bar exam. Some students become excessively worried about the exam. You shouldn't be. If you passed my class, the bar exam is a stroll in a park. Anyone can pass, if they approach the exam correctly. Here's how.

Preparing for the Bar Exam

Too many graduating law students fail to properly prepare for the bar exam. Many take the exam seriously, but some students each year appear to believe the exam is overly easy. While it's not a complicated exam, it does require lots of preparation. After all of the work and stress of law school, the bar exam is not the time to let up.

A. Have the Right Mindset

You can pass the bar exam on your first attempt, but you must approach preparing for the exam with the right mindset. First, you must take it seriously. Passing a bar exam is as much about commitment as it is about learning substantive law. Never take a bar exam for "practice" or as a "trial run." Sitting for the exam with the intent to take it again will become a self-fulfilling prophecy. You must commit to working hard and passing the exam the first time. Second, you need to approach the exam with a positive attitude, knowing you will pass if you prepare properly. Students who have earned a J.D. from an accredited school have the skills necessary to pass the exam the first time. That's true even for the most notoriously difficult bar exams: California and New York.

B. Focus in Law School

The best preparation for the bar exam occurs in law school. For most law schools there exists a strong correlation between class rank and bar pass rate. Students who do well in law school pass at higher rates than students who have performed poorly. This does not mean that students with low GPAs will fail the bar exam, but they are at a greater risk. So engaging and doing your best in law school is a good way to get prepared for the bar exam.

Be certain to enroll in rigorous courses that force you to write, to think analytically, and to master complicated legal issues.

Bar preparation courses that you take while studying for the bar exam do not adequately teach you how to write an exam essay or do legal analysis. Bar preparation courses will usually teach you the black letter law of the topics tested comprehensively, but those courses provide very little in the way of how to write, or how to analyze — you are assumed to have learned those skills in law school.

Many schools now have a variety of programs and workshops that are designed to help you pass the exam your first time. The ABA now permits law schools to offer bar preparation courses for credit. If your school offers those programs, you should take advantage of them.

C. Understand the Exam Structure

Each state has a different exam requirements, but most exams are roughly similar. Typically, a bar exam will be two days, with a few states having three-day exams. One day is devoted to multiple choice questions, and the other days are devoted to different kinds of essays. Some states have short essays, others long, and some states have small sets of multiple choice questions related to specific topics of law.

Each day of the bar exam usually involves six hours of testing (three hours in the morning, three hours in the afternoon). With the exception of a few states, the Multistate Bar Exam (MBE) occupies one full day. The MBE portion of the exam consists of 200 multiple choice questions on the following subjects: civil procedure, contracts, torts, constitutional law, criminal law and procedure, evidence, and real property.

Most states will also require that students complete a day of essay exams. Some states, such as California, also utilize a performance exam. A performance exam is designed to be a realistic situation that an attorney might encounter early in their career. For each question, the applicant receives a case file and a library (a collection of statutes and cases). The applicant is then assigned a task, such as writing an opinion letter, or a brief, or a memo, or a closing argument.

In addition to the bar exam itself, many states require that candidates pass the Multistate Professional Responsibility Exam (MPRE) before being admitted to practice. The MPRE is a 125-minute exam, consisting of 60 multiple choice questions. The exam is administered three times a year in March, August, and November. Generally, students should take the MPRE well in advance of the bar exam.

D. Meet Deadlines

Each state has its own requirements. Before a student's last year in law school — as much as twelve to fourteen months before graduation — students should know what they must do to become licensed in the state in which they intend to practice. Each state has their own requirements (including, among other things, registering, as well as submitting an application, fingerprint cards, and a moral character petition, etc.). Fortunately, most states have websites that provide detailed information about the requirements to practice law.

You should pay close attention to deadlines. The application process can be expensive, and submitting a late application will increase the fees significantly. In several states, a late application fee can nearly double the cost of the application. You also need to be careful not to miss deadlines to submit requests to type the exam on your laptop or for disability accommodations. For most states, the bar application is due several months before a student graduates. Many states also require that students meet certain "moral character and fitness" requirements. This process may require letters of reference and possibly interviews. Although requirements vary among jurisdictions, you must ensure that you complete all required paperwork on time.

E. Prepare Financially

The bar exam is expensive. The costs of submitting an application and completing a preparation course will for many jurisdictions be thousands of dollars. Graduating students often borrow money to finance the costs of bar exam registration, exam-related preparatory materials, and the living expenses during the two months from graduation to the date of the exam. This is known as a "bridge" or "bar" loan. Most school's financial aid offices have information for students about sources of funding for bridge loans. At the start of your last year of law school, make an appointment with a financial aid counselor at your school to see what options may be available to you.

You should do your best to get your finances in order so that you do not have to work while studying for the exam. Studying for the exam is a full-time job. For many exams — like the California and New York exams — working while studying for the exam is difficult and will significantly increase your chances of failure. If you do need to work while preparing for the exam, you should have a frank discussion with your employer about what time you will need off to study.

This is also not the time to shy away from a loan. Taking out a bar study loan and studying full-time is much cheaper than working while studying and then failing. Not passing on your first attempt means at least six more months of not being an attorney, as well as incurring the costs of having to pay another bar registration fee and take another bar preparation course.

F. Research Preparation Courses

In your last year of law school (or perhaps earlier), you should carefully research and determine which commercial bar preparation course you will be taking. Taking a commercial preparation course is not optional. For almost all jurisdictions it's essential to passing the bar exam. You should take a preparation course.

You want to weigh a number of factors before deciding on a bar preparation course. For different courses ask yourself, what is the cost? How often do the classes meet? Who teaches the course? How is instruction provided? How is feedback provided and how does the course assess your progress? Is the course comprehensive? What is the success rate for students taking the course? Does the course's approach fit your learning style? There are many good commercial preparation courses, but there also some very poor ones. Be sure to do the research ahead of time so that you feel comfortable with the decision you've made. Talk to others (hopefully friends you trust) who have recently taken the course. Get a sense of what they liked and disliked.

The courses are expensive — usually several thousands of dollars — so you want to ensure you've done your research. Be wary of courses that cost several thousand dollars more than other courses in your jurisdiction. If a commercial bar preparation course promises something that sounds too good to be true, it probably is.

G. Prepare Your Life

From the time you graduate until you take the bar exam — approximately two months — you need to study ten or more hours a day, at least six days a week. To focus solely on the exam during those two months, you must get your life in order. Take care of any errands that you would otherwise do (e.g., getting your car fixed, seeing the dentist or the doctor, taking your pet to the vet). Remove as many distractions from your life as possible.

Tell your family and friends how important this exam is. You must explain that you will be mostly unavailable for the two months leading up to the exam. The two months that you are studying for the exam is also not the time to be making any major changes in your life. This is not the time to have surgery, take a vacation, get married or divorced, move homes, or start a new relationship.

If you are a parent, also plan for your children. If you have young children, be certain to arrange for child care and back-up child care. For your children's sake, make sure to factor time to spend with your children into your study schedule. You need to study, but family is important too.

H. Petition for Accommodations

Most states provide reasonable accommodations for applicants with documented disabilities. If you have received special accommodations for exams during law schools, you should attempt to get those same accommodations for the bar exam. Each jurisdiction, however, has its own procedures for determining whether an applicant is permitted exam accommodations. If you have a physical or learning disability be certain to submit the testing accommodation forms early. You must also ensure that you have sufficient documentation to support the accommodation.

Studying for the Bar Exam

Not only is it important that you prepare for the bar exam, but during the approximately two months between graduation and the exam you must study properly. Here's how:

A. Take a Preparation Course

Commercial bar preparation courses are a must. They are not optional. There are many good courses out there, with many different teaching styles. Pick one.

Once you have picked one, be sure to do exactly what they tell you and follow their study plans. Be sure to follow the advice they give precisely. If they tell you to take a practice exam, take a practice exam. If they tell you to read an outline, read the outline. If they tell you to take 50 MBE (multiple choice) questions a day, take 50 MBE questions a day. You are paying a lot of money to have them help you pass the exam. You should follow their advice exactly.

B. Create a Schedule

To pass most bar exams you must learn and memorize a large number of rules, take many practice exams, and attend bar review courses. You need to plan for how you will get it all done. Schedule what you will do every day for each week. The schedule should be detailed, indicating exactly when you will attend your bar preparation course and listen to lectures, when you will take practice exams, when you'll practice MBE questions, and when you will review your notes and outlines. Generally you should get up early and do your most difficult studying first. You should schedule in time to exercise, take breaks, and eat. You will need to take a periodic evening or afternoon off, and may need to schedule time to spend with your spouse, children or other loved ones. Schedule it all. Stick to your schedule.

Two scheduling tips. First, consider scheduling 10 MBEs to do right when you wake up in the morning and 10 MBEs as you get in bed for the evening. If you can get into this routine, it is an easy way to lighten your load the rest of the day and break up the work. Second, avoid saving all your written essays for the end of the day. The essays are hard. They take a lot of brain power. You should practice at least one essay while you have energy. The longer you put it off, the more likely you are to skip it.

C. Study Ten to Twelve Hours a Day

Each jurisdiction is different, and the difficulty of the exams vary widely. But as a rule of thumb, studying for the bar exam requires studying ten to twelve hours each day, five or six days a week. For most bar exams, the amount of material you need to learn during the two months leading up to the exam is voluminous. To master all the material and take sufficient practice exams requires studying full time. This means for most exams you should plan on studying ten to twelve hours a day or more. When studying, be sure to work steadily.

D. Study Actively, Not Passively

You will not pass the bar exam if you spend all your time memorizing outlines, flashcards, or notes. If you devote your study time to reviewing notes and memorizing rules, you increase your chance of failure. You need to practice real bar questions to learn how the rules actually work on the exam. Only by taking MBE practice questions and writing out actual essay exams will you train yourself to spot issues. You can master the elements of assault and intentional infliction of emotional distress and still miss key issues in an essay question. If the essay says the defendant yelled at the plaintiff, "I am going to kill you," you might naturally think to discuss intentional infliction of emotional distress, but forget to address assault even though you knew the elements. You might assume you don't need to discuss assault because there was no physical action by the defendant. You learn from taking the practice question that both issues need to be addressed, even if only to state that the elements of assault are not met. By taking the essays, you not only learn the black letter law, you learn when and how to address each issue.

To have the best chance of success on the bar exam, you must learn actively. You should take 1000s of MBE practice questions (literally), and write out many practice essay exams. As a general rule, you should answer at least 40–50 practice MBE a day and write at least one (hopefully two) sample essay exams each day. This is in addition to the hours spent in your bar class listening to lectures. Do not wait until you know the black letter law to take practice exams. Instead, learn the law by taking the practice exams. If you still have time for reading outlines after completing at least 40 MBEs and 1–2 essays, go for it.

When you take a practice exam, it is important that you assess how you're doing. Be sure to review your answer carefully and analyze what you did well and what you need to improve. One effective way to actively review your answer is to journal every rule you miss (on both MBE questions and essay questions) into a notebook. Do not journal by typing the rules on your laptop or voicing them into an app. Actually handwrite them. It is the process of physically handwriting the rules that make them stick. The purpose of journaling is not to create a tool to review the rules you missed. You are not likely to go back and read the journal. Thus, you don't have to worry about how you organize the rules you write in your journal. The purpose of the journal is to write the rules down so you are active in working with the rules. You will be surprised how frequently you remember a rule just by writing the rule down one time.

For optimal retention of the material, you should take MBEs in sets of ten. Take ten questions, then review all ten (even if you got them right). Any rule you did not know gets written in your journal. Completing only ten MBEs at a time is key to efficiency. If you take more than ten questions at a time, you will forget the first question by the time you go back to review it, and you will need to re-read the question. However, if you stop after ten questions to review, you are likely to remember the questions and can quickly look through the explanation of the answers. This will help you keep on schedule. In addition, if you only do only ten MBEs at a time, you are more likely to actually complete the review process (which is key to you learning the material). If you complete fifty MBEs at a time, the review process simply becomes too daunting.

E. Take Timed Practice Exams

Equally important as taking practice exams is to take some of those exams timed. Although your regular practice should involve fewer MBE questions at a time, once a week take 200 multiple choice questions under real timed conditions. You need to build up stamina to complete the bar exam. You would not walk out the door thinking you could run a marathon if you had only practiced running a mile each day. Similarly, you cannot expect your brain to operate effectively for three hours if you have not trained it to do so. Once a week (or at least once every other week), practice completing 200 MBE questions under "real life conditions." After you have taken the exam, be certain to assess how you did. You will not be able to review all 200 MBE questions, but at least review the ones you missed. Apply this same logic to essays and, if applicable, performance exams. At least a few times during your preparation, practice writing three essay questions in three hours.

F. Manage Your Environment

When studying for the bar exam or taking practice exams, ensure that you are in a comfortable place without distractions. Ideally you should be in a place where you have enough room to stretch out: where you can place your outlines, and notes, and bar review materials. Before beginning, think ahead so you have what you need for the next hour. You don't want to be jumping up every few minutes to get a book, or a pen, or another cup of coffee. You also want to ensure you're not too close to friends. The bar exam is not the time to be catching up on the latest gossip. You have to focus on concentrated studying.

G. Stay Healthy

Managing stress and reducing anxiety is critical for doing well. When you're stressed you do not retain and remember the material you're studying, and studying becomes inefficient. Exercise is a valuable way to reduce stress. So too is staying healthy by eating good food on a regular basis. Get plenty of sleep. In short, use common sense and stay as healthy as you can.

Answering Bar Exam Questions

How do you answer a bar exam essay question? Usually the same way you answered law school exam essay questions. Here's a reminder of the key points:

A. Use IRAC

To pass the bar exam, you must demonstrate your ability to use legal analysis and organize your answer. When answering questions on the bar exam, use IRAC — Issue, Rule, Analysis/Application, Conclusion. For each question asked, spot the relevant issues, explain what rules relate to those issues, use the facts that are relevant to the issues to make arguments, and draw a reasoned conclusion. You must make a logical and reasoned argument that explains why the facts show that certain elements or rules have been met or not met. Remember, applying the facts does not mean simply restating the facts or regurgitating the question. Also, do not omit key facts assuming the reader knows them. You must show your work, and explain your thought process in a logical way.

You want the bar exam grader to understand your analysis easily and quickly. Write each part of the IRAC as a separate paragraph. Here's a sample answer to a bar exam evidence essay question, with each part of the IRAC labeled.

A. Is Paul's Statement "I Shot Him" Inadmissible Hearsay [Call of the Question]

Hearsay [Issue]

Hearsay is (i) an out-of-court statement (ii) used to prove the truth of the matter asserted. Hearsay is inadmissible unless an exception to the hearsay rule applies. [Rule]

Here, the statement "I shot him" was an out-of-court statement because Paul made the statement at a nightclub and not in a court room under oath. The statement is also being used to prove the truth of the matter asserted because the prosecutor is trying to establish that Paul is guilty of murder for killing John, the victim, who died from a gunshot wound. The statement "I shot him" is therefore being used to prove that Paul in fact shot John rather than for some other purpose. [Analysis]

Both elements of hearsay are met. Thus, Paul's statement is hearsay and would be inadmissible unless an exception applies. [Conclusion]

Notice how the heading serves as the "I" of the IRAC. The "R" section clearly sets forth the elements of the law and is contained in its own paragraph. All relevant rules are addressed within that one paragraph. No new rules appear below in the application. The "A" is also contained in its own paragraph and properly uses the "because" format to apply facts to the law. The application uses the exact wording of the rule (out-of-court statement) and links it to the specific facts of the case (made at a nightclub) using the word "because." Finally, the "C" is set forth separately in its own paragraph and concludes on the overall legal issue (hearsay). Breaking the analysis up this way makes the answer easy to read and grade.

When drafting your essays for the bar exam, follow the same strategies and formatting rules as discussed for taking law school exams in Chapter 6. With respect to formatting: calls of the question in bold, each main legal issue underlined, subheadings underlined and indented. Avoid sub-subheadings where possible and never have sub-sub-sub headings.

B. Allocate Your Time

Just as with law school exams, allocating your time is critical. If the bar exam gives you three hours to write three essays, you must spend no more than one hour on each essay. The reason for this is simple: you must pass all the portions of the exam. Doing very well on one essay question and very poorly on another question will lead to a failing grade. As soon as your allocated time has expired — even if you're not finished with your answer — you must move on to the next question. If you have time left over at the end of the exam, you can go back to earlier questions.

C. Approach the Essay Exam Methodically

As with law school exams, you should approach the essay question methodically. First, read the call of the question. What is the question asking? What area of the law is implicated? Take 3–5 minutes to just spend time thinking about the question so you don't accidently write about the wrong thing. Type the calls of the questions into your outline and bold them. Don't lose sight of them and make sure to spend time addressing all calls of the question.

Second, read the fact pattern carefully. Then, read the fact pattern again and start outlining. During your second read of the fact pattern, you should have legal issues popping into your head. Start typing them into your outline. Each time a legal issue comes to mind, type it into your outline. As you read the facts, fill in the relevant facts where they fit into the legal issues. Some facts may fit into more than one issue. Spend about ten, maybe even fifteen minutes, completing this process. Do not start writing until you have thought through what main issues are implicated by the question and how you intend to organize your answer.

After outlining the issue and facts, start writing your answer. Fill in the rules and application for each heading/sub-heading you have created. Your facts will already be typed within each heading — make sure you use them. Use them exactly. You need to use the specific facts from the exam answer. Don't summarize them. Be sure to stop writing and move on once the time you've allocated for the question is up.

D. Remember to Use the Word Because

As with law school exams, it is critical that you explain how you reach your conclusions. A conclusion without a reason does not make a passing bar exam answer. Link the exact wording of the rule to the facts of the essay using the word *because*. To pass the bar exam, you must demonstrate that you understand how to apply legal concepts in particular factual circumstances to reach a probable conclusion.

E. Argue Both Sides

For many (but not all) of the issues raised by a bar exam question, you must explain what the strongest arguments are for each side. If you think the plaintiff will win, what is the strongest argument for the defendant? If you think a legal element is met, what is the strongest argument that it is not met? Be sure to highlight to bar examiners when the questions asked are "close calls." Remember the approaches to organizing counter-arguments for law school exams? Same ideas apply here. There are different approaches to organizing counter-arguments, but starting with the weaker argument first saves times because it avoids the requirement to include a rebuttal. Remember, only some of the issues on the bar exam call for counter-arguments. Only raise a counter-argument if there are facts to support it.

Some Practicalities

Doing well on the bar exam requires mastering anxiety and ensuring that you are not distracted during the exam period. To help with managing stress and anxiety and to give yourself the best chance of succeeding, consider doing the following:

A. Reserve a Hotel Room

Do not commute long distances to the bar exam. Be certain to book a hotel room near the examination site (close enough to walk to and from the hotel). Rooms often fill up quickly near exam sites, so book early. As soon as you find out where you are taking the exam, make a reservation.

Avoid sharing rooms with others: you need a quiet place to unwind each night of the exam.

If you are unable to stay in a hotel during the exam or would prefer to stay at home, be certain to know ahead of time how to get to the exam site, and where to park if you are driving. If you are commuting, do a dry run during rush hour so you know exactly how long it will take to get to the exam site. If you are commuting, be sure to leave early. If you are driving, you might consider carpooling (or at least have a back-up if something happens to your car).

B. Tie Up Loose Ends

Think ahead. If you have children, be certain that you have arranged for child care. If you have pets, make sure you have someone who can look after them during the two or three days of the exam. If you are taking the exam using a laptop, ensure that your laptop is working properly. Pack the supplies you will take to the exam ahead of time (such as pens, pencils, highlighters, aspirin, a timer, etc.).

C. Visit the Exam Site

You do not want to be worrying about where you need to go on the day of the exam. Visit where you are taking the exam long before exam day. Make sure you know where you're going and how to get there.

D. Pack Ahead of Time

The day or night before the bar exam is not the time to pack. Be sure to pack ahead of time so that you don't forget anything you need. If the exam permits a silent timer, do you have one? An alarm clock that works? Your laptop? Have you packed sufficient pens, pencils, and highlighters? Do you have comfortable clothes? Perhaps you might even pack snacks. Think through what you need and pack ahead of time. Also, to prevent unpleasant surprises, read the exams instruction very carefully so you know exactly what is permitted in the exam room.

The Day of the Bar Exam

Not only should you prepare ahead of time, you should also keep in mind what you will need on the first day of the exam.

A. Wear Comfortable Clothes

A bar exam is not a fashion show. Don't worry about how you look. Nobody cares at the bar exam. Wear your most comfortable clothes, and wear them in layers. The air conditioning or heating may be blasting, or not working at all. Layers will allow you to respond to any conditions.

B. Eat Breakfast, Lunch, and Dinner

Be sure to eat during breaks in the exam. For breakfast you do not want something heavy — this is not time for the lumberjack special with a double side of sausage and bacon — but it will be a long day and you need to eat something.

Plan ahead. For some exam testing centers in large cities, there may be hundreds of students taking the exam at the same time. In those cases, it may be difficult to eat at a nearby restaurant during the allocated lunch break. Consider packing lunch. It may save you some unnecessary stress and put you in a better position for the afternoon portion of the exam.

C. Arrive Early

Much of the key to passing the bar exam is managing stress. You cannot do well on the exam if you panic. To reduce stress, be sure to arrive early. Check in. Get a good seat (if the examiners don't assign one to you). Get focused. You will not be permitted to take the exam if you arrive late. So don't make it close. Get to the exam site with plenty of time to spare.

D. Leave Your Study Materials

You cannot cram for the bar exam. Doing so is a waste of time. Do not bother trying to learn anything new right before the exam. You'll just cause yourself unnecessary stress. So leave your study materials at home or in the hotel room.

E. Expect the Unexpected

No matter how much you have prepared, something unexpected can happen. Urban myths are chock full of "bar exam stories": earthquakes disrupting exams, broken heaters leading to sauna-like exam conditions, students breaking out in hives, students running screaming from the exam room, rock bands banging away next door.... Your testing center is likely to have some distractions you were not expecting. Don't let it rattle you. Expect the unexpected. Deal with it. Ignore it. Focus on the exam.

F. Do Not Discuss the Exam

If you followed my advice from first year, don't ignore it now. During the exam, do not discuss specific bar exam questions with others. You will be tempted to do so, but don't. Discussing the substance of bar exam will only lead to increasing your stress. Keep your conversations generic.

G. Don't Obsess

When it's over, forget about the exam. You will have answered some questions right and some questions wrong. You didn't need to ace the exam to pass, and students are terrible at predicting whether they passed. So don't even try. This is not the time to second guess how you did. In fact, do not think about the exam again until the results are released (several months later). If you have the flexibility, this is a good time to take a vacation. At the very least, try not to go back to work the very next day. You'll be tired. Maybe even exhausted. This is the time to rest. You've earned it.

―――――――――

As you embark on your journey to take one of the biggest tests you will ever take, I'll leave you with this: Study. Study hard. Make it your full time job. All crankiness aside, you will be fine. You can do this. Believe in yourself. You are ready to be a lawyer.

Checklist Reminders

Basic Preparation for the Bar Exam

❑ *Focus and work hard in law school (all three years, not just the first!)*
❑ *Take any preparation programs that the school offers*
❑ *Figure out the exam's structure (how many essays, MBE questions, or performance tests)*
❑ *Pay close attention to application deadlines*
❑ *Prepare financially and meet with school's financial aid office*
❑ *Research the different kinds of commercial bar preparation courses available*
❑ *Clear the decks after graduation to study only for the bar exam*

Studying for the Bar Exam

- ❏ Take a preparation courses (not optional, a must!)
- ❏ Do exactly what the preparation course tells you to do
- ❏ Create a study schedule for the two months leading up to the exam — and stick with it
- ❏ Study ten to twelve hours a day (sometimes more)
- ❏ Study actively (lots and lots of practice exams)
- ❏ Take timed practice exams
- ❏ Study in a quiet, distraction-free place
- ❏ Stay healthy — eat and exercise
- ❏ Rely on friends and family

Writing Bar Exam Essays

- ❏ Use IRAC
- ❏ Allocate time between questions
- ❏ Approach the exam methodically (read the call, read the facts, outline an answer)
- ❏ Explain your conclusions — use the word "because"
- ❏ Argue both sides when necessary
- ❏ Move on to next question when allocated time is up (even if not finished)

Practicalities Before the Exam

- ❏ Reserve a hotel room well in advance
- ❏ Tie up loose ends; get personal life in order
- ❏ Visit the exam site
- ❏ Pack ahead of time
- ❏ Figure out where to eat lunch, dinner at exam site

The Day of the Exam

- ❏ Wear comfortable clothes
- ❏ Eat breakfast, lunch, and dinner (need food to think properly)
- ❏ Arrive to exam early
- ❏ Leave study materials at home (no cramming!)
- ❏ Prepare mentally to expect the unexpected
- ❏ Never discuss the substance of the exam with friends
- ❏ Don't obsess once it's over

CONCLUSION

What? You want more? Are you kidding me?! Time to graduate.

SELECTED BIBLIOGRAPHY

A. General Advice

Paul Bergman, Patrick Goodman, & Thomas Holm, *Cracking the Case Method* (2d ed. 2017)

Ann Burkhart & Robert Stein, *Law School Success in a Nutshell* (3rd ed. 2017)

Atticus Falcon, *Planet Law School II: What You Need to Know (Before You Go), But Didn't Know to Ask, and No One Else Will Tell You* (2d ed. 2003)

Ursula Furi-Perry, *Law School Revealed: Secrets, Opportunities, and Success!* (2009)

Rebecca Fae Greene, *Law School for Dummies* (2003)

Jeremy B. Horwitz, *Law School Insider: The Comprehensive 21st Century Guide* (2002)

Ann L. Iijima, *The Law Student's Pocket Mentor: From Surviving to Thriving* (2007)

Andrew J. McClurg, *1L of a Ride: A Well-Traveled Professor's Roadmap to Success in the First Year of Law School* (3rd ed. 2017)

Robert H. Miller, *Law School Confidential: A Complete Guide to the Law School Experience: By Students, for Students* (2004)

Gary A. Munneke, *How to Succeed in Law School* (4th ed. 2008)

Shana Connell Noyes & Henry S. Noyes, *Acing Your First Year of Law School: The Ten Steps to Success You Won't Learn in Class* (2d ed. 2008)

Herbert Ramy, *Succeeding in Law School* (3d ed. 2020)

Steven Sedberry, *Law School Labyrinth*: *A Guide to Making the Most of Your Legal Education* (3d ed. 2015)

Ira L. Shafiroff, *First-Year Law School Success: The Ultimate and Essential Guide for Every 1L* (4th ed. 2018)

Helene Shapo & Marshall Shapo, *Law School Without Fear*: *Strategies for Success* (3d ed. 2009)

B. Final Exams

Charles Calleros, *Law School Exams: Preparing and Writing to Win* (2d ed. 2013)

John C. Dernbach, *Writing Essay Exams to Succeed* (4th ed. 2014)

Richard Michael Fischl et al., *Getting to Maybe: How to Excel on Law School Exams* (1999)

Alex Schimel, Law School Exams: A Guide to Better Grades (2d ed. 2018)

Charles H. Whitebread, *The Eight Secrets to Top Exam Performance in Law School* (2d ed. 2007)

C. Learning and Reading

Ruth Anne McKinney, *Reading Like a Lawyer: Time-Saving Strategies for Reading Law Like an Expert* (2d ed. 2012)

Michael Hunter Schwartz & Paula J. Manning, *Expert Learning for Law Student* (3d ed. 2018)

Elizabeth Mertz, *The Language of Law School: Learning to Think Like a Lawyer* (2007)

D. Miscellaneous

Mary Basick & Tina Schindler, *Essay Exam Writing for the California Bar Exam* (2d ed. 2010)

Mary Basick & Tina Schindler, *MBE Decoded — Multistate Bar Exam* (2021)

Barbara K. Bucholtz et al., *The Little Black Book: A Do-It-Yourself Guide to Law Student Competitions* (2002)

Rachel Gader-Shafron, *The International Students' Survival Guide to Law School in the United States* (2003)

Linda R. Hirshman, *The Women's Guide to Law School* (1999)

James E. Moliterno & Frederic I. Lederer, *An Introduction to Law, Law Study, and the Lawyer's Role* (3d ed. 2010)

Jay M. Feinman, *Law 101: Everything You Need Know About the American Legal System* (2d ed. 2006)

Steven J. Frank, *Learning the Law: Success in Law School and Beyond* (2d ed. 2000)

Kenney F. Hegland, *Introduction to the Study of Law in a Nutshell* (8th ed. 2020)

Ruta K. Stropus & Charlotte D. Taylor, *Bridging the Gap Between College and Law School: Strategies for Success* (3d ed. 2014)

SAMPLE CASE BRIEF

A. A Sample Decision

Below is an edited version of the California Court of Appeal decision in *People v. Corson*, 34 Cal. Rptr. 584 (Ct. App. 1963). After the decision is a sample case brief.

District Court of Appeal, Third District, California.

The PEOPLE of the State of California, Plaintiff and Respondent,
v.
Harry CORSON, Defendant and Appellant.
Cr. 3484.
Oct. 28, 1963.
Rehearing Denied Nov. 26, 1963.

Defendant was convicted before the Superior Court, Trinity County, Harold Underwood, J., of assault with a deadly weapon, and he appealed. The District Court of Appeal, Schottky, J., held that fact that defendant might have been intoxicated either through use of liquor or mixture of liquor and pills was no defense to prosecution for assault with deadly weapon.

Judgment affirmed.

Harry L. Corson in pro. per.
Stanley Mosk, Atty. Gen., by Doris Maier, Asst. Atty. Gen., and John Giordano, Deputy Atty. Gen., Sacramento, for respondent.

SCHOTTKY, Justice.

Harry Corson was charged by information with the crime of assault with a deadly weapon. He was found guilty as charged by a jury, probation was denied, and judgment was pronounced sentencing him to a term in the state prison. He has appealed from the judgment entered.

The factual situation as shown by the record may be summarized as follows: Corson and his wife lived in a house on a ranch owned by Melvin Senna in Trinity County. On the morning of September 4, 1961, Corson and his wife took a truck of Senna's to go into town to attend to certain errands. When the Corsons failed to return, Senna went to town to learn the cause of the delay. Senna found his truck parked outside a bar. He went to the entrance and saw Corson and his wife sitting at the bar and he told them he was taking the truck. Mrs. Corson came out and asked for a ride back to the ranch. Corson came out and attempted to pull his wife from the vehicle. Senna pulled Corson away. Senna returned to his ranch. About 6:30 p. m. Howard Palmer drove Corson to his house on the ranch. Palmer then drove his car up the road to where Senna was standing and told Senna and Mrs. Corson, 'Harry's really pushed out of shape. [H]e's going to shoot you.' Senna then saw Corson come out of his house armed with a double barreled shotgun. Corson shouted that

he was going to kill the 'Portugee.' He broke the gun when he shouted and loaded it. Corson then started walking toward Senna. Senna got into Palmer's truck and was driven to his cabin. He entered his house, got his rifle and returned to the front porch, where he shouted to Corson to stop. Corson continued to walk toward Senna with the shotgun pointed in Senna's direction. Senna fired a warning shot over Corson's head and told Corson not to come any closer. Corson turned around and walked back to his house. When Senna fired the shot Corson was about 175 feet away. The deputy sheriff who arrested Corson testified that he found Corson's shotgun loaded with two shells.

Corson testified in his own defense. The main point of his testimony was that he had taken six pain or nerve pills during the day; that he had not eaten anything; that he drank beer and was pretty drunk. He contended he blacked out. He testified that he could not recollect picking up his shotgun, loading it or walking toward Senna. Corson claimed that the first he could recall was the firing of the shot. He recalled telling Senna he missed and turning around. His next recollection was the arrival of the deputy sheriff.

Section 245 of the Penal Code makes it a crime to commit an assault upon the person of another with a deadly weapon or instrument.

An assault is an unlawful attempt, coupled with a present ability, to commit a violent injury on the person of another. (Pen. Code, sec. 240.) To constitute an assault there must be a specific intent to commit a battery, and an act which is close to accomplishment and not mere preparation. (1 Witkin, Cal. Crimes, Assault, sec. 256, p. 242.)

Appellant has filed a brief in propria persona and makes a number of contentions, the first of which is that the evidence is not sufficient to support the conviction of assault with a deadly weapon because, so he contends, there is no evidence that appellant had any intention of causing anybody great bodily injury.

The applicable law is set forth in People v. Roshid, 'All that is required to sustain a conviction of assault with a deadly weapon is proof that there was an assault, that it was with a deadly weapon, and that the defendant intended to commit a violent injury on another. Pen.Code, §245; People v. Marcus, 133 Cal. App.2d 579, 581, 284 P.2d 848. An assault is an unlawful attempt, coupled with a present ability, to commit a violent injury on the person of another. Pen.Code, §240. A gun capable of being fired is a deadly weapon. People v. Pittullo, 116 Cal. App.2d 373, 376, 253 P.2d 705. The intent may be inferred from the doing of the wrongful act. People v. Walker, 99 Cal.App.2d 238, 242, 221 P.2d 287.' (See also People v. McCoy, 25 Cal.2d 177, 189, 153 P.2d 315.)

We think it is clear there was ample evidence that there was an unlawful attempt, coupled with the present ability, to commit a violent injury on the person of Mr. Senna. The record indicates that the appellant came out of his house carrying a shotgun. Standing on the porch in full view of Mr. Senna, Mr. and Mrs. Palmer and Mrs. Corson, the appellant loaded the gun, yelled that he was going to kill the 'Portugee,' and then started walking toward Mr. Senna in a 'stalking' manner and only halted when Mr. Senna finally fired a warning shot into the air. There clearly was an assault. The loaded shotgun in question is well within the meaning of 'deadly weapon or instrument' of section 245 of the Penal Code.

Appellant further contends that due to his intoxicated condition he could not have had any intent to injure Mr. Senna. The law is clear that the intent necessary in this type of case may be inferred from the doing of the wrongful act. (Citations omitted).

The fact that the appellant may have been intoxicated either by the liquor he consumed or by a mixture of the liquor and the 'pills' he claims he took is no defense. 'No act committed by a person while in a state of voluntary intoxication is less criminal by reason of his having been in such condition.' (Pen. Code, sec. 22.) Voluntary intoxication, whether induced by liquor or drugs, is not a defense. (Citations omitted).

The judgment is affirmed.

PIERCE, P. J., and FRIEDMAN, J., concur.

B. Case Brief

PEOPLE v. CORSON
34 Cal. Rptr. 584 (Ct. App. 1963)

ISSUE:

Under California law, is a defendant guilty of assault with a deadly weapon when he grabs a double-barreled shotgun, loads it, and shouts that he is "going to kill the [victim]" before being stopped, if at the time the defendant is intoxicated after drinking beer and taking pain pills?

FACTS:

Corson lived with his wife on a ranch that Senna owned. One day Corson took Senna's truck to town. When Corson did not return, Senna investigated and found Corson drinking at a bar. Corson had taken six pain pills, had not eaten anything, and drank beer until he "was pretty drunk." Senna drove the truck and Corson's wife back to the ranch.

That evening, after Corson returned to the ranch, he came out of his house armed with a double-barreled shotgun. Corson loaded the gun, and shouted to Senna that he was going to kill him. Corson then started walking in a "stalking manner" towards Senna. Senna had previously been told that Corson was "really pushed out of shape.... [and was] going to shoot [Senna]." Senna retrieved his own gun, shot a warning shot over Corson's head, and told Corson not to come any closer. Corson turned around and walked back to his house. Later, Corson was arrested.

PROCEDURE:

Corson was charged with, convicted of, and sentenced for assaulting Senna with a deadly weapon. Corson appealed. He contended: (1) that his actions did not constitute assault because there was no evidence he intended to cause anyone great bodily injury; and (2) because of his intoxication, he could not have had the intent to injure Senna.

LEGAL RULES:

1. Assault is an unlawful attempt, coupled with a present ability, to commit a violent injury. Cal. Penal Code § 240. 2. Committing an assault with a deadly weapon or instrument is a crime. Cal. Penal Code § 245. 3. "No act committed by a person while in a state of voluntary intoxication is less criminal by reason of his having been in such a condition." Cal. Penal Code § 22.

HOLDING:

The defendant was guilty of assault with a deadly weapon. The defendant's voluntarily intoxicated was no defense to prosecution for the assault.

REASONING:

First, a gun capable of being fired is a deadly weapon. A loaded shotgun is within the meaning of "deadly weapon or instrument" of section 245. Second, carrying a shot gun, loading it, threatening to kill a person, and then walking towards that person is ample evidence of an intent to injure another. Under the statute and case-law, voluntary intoxication is not a defense.

SAMPLE OUTLINES

The following three sample outlines are small portions of a larger contracts outline. Do not use these sample outlines as your own outlines for class. Rather, you must incorporate the rules that your professor teaches and adopt an organization that works with your professor's lessons. The purpose of creating an outline is to grapple with how the different rules fit together. It is the struggle of fitting the rules together that really makes you to learn them. Use these samples merely as examples.

Sample Portion of a Contracts Outline
Formation of a Contract

I. What law applies to contracts?
   1. **UCC applies:** contract involves sale of goods (moveable items)
   2. **Common Law applies:** contract involves services or real estate
   3. **Mixed between goods and services:** look to predominant purpose

II. Is a Contract Formed?
   1. **Mutual Assent**
      a. Must be a meeting of the minds (the parties must agree upon the specifics of the bargain)
         i. *A makes an offer to sell B his car for $10,000. B states that he accepts the offer. Mutual assent has arisen through a process of offer and acceptance*
      b. Look to the offers and acceptance

   c. Measure using an objectively reasonable person standard
      i. *Lucy v. Zehmer* — parties talk about selling a farm; agree on a price; later the seller says he was just kidding; court says there was a valid contract because seller's outward expression was that he wanted to sell the farm; need to look at what the parties say/do rather than what they subjectively intend

2. **Consideration**
   d. **Bargained for exchange** — each party giving up something and receiving something in return
      i. the Promisee must suffer a legal detriment
      ii. the detriment must induce the promise
      iii. the promise must induce the detriment
   e. **Amount of consideration does not matter**
      i. Don't need equivalence between what is promised and what the detriment is (unless it is clearly a gift, like paying $10 for a beach house)
      ii. *Gottlieb v. Tropicana* — pl enrolled in a membership program that allowed one free slot machine spin; she spins and wins $1 million; court said there was consideration, even if it's as slight as giving information to enroll in the membership program or standing in line (peppercorn will suffice)
   f. **No consideration for:**
      i. Gifts
      ii. Past consideration (need to engage in a current act)
      iii. Illusory promises ("I will buy this if I feel like it")
      iv. Output/requirement contracts
      v. Pre-Existing Duty Rule: when an obligation already exists under the existing K and there was no furnishing of additional consideration

3. **Offer**
   g. A valid offer is one that invites acceptance from OE and indicates that assent will conclude the bargain
   h. It must be directed towards a specific person

     i. *Craft case — advertisements are not offers, but rather an invitation to negotiate*
- Defendant Craft advertised the sale of a sewing machine; plaintiff went to buy it but def refused to fulfill the offer in the ad; the court sided with defs stating that an ad is not an offer since it is made to the public generally

     ii. *Lefkowitz case — look for definitive terms and/or promissory words*
- An ad for one wool coat was an offer since the ad was definitive as to the quantity and worth, it included promissory words like "first come, first serve" and left nothing open for negotiation

     iii. *Pepsico case — look to whether the offer was made in jest/joke*
- TV commercial showed a commercial jet for points collected from purchasing Pepsi; the pl raised money and bought millions of points and demanded the jet; the court sided with def and said the advertisement for the jet was not an offer since an objective reasonable person would know it was a joke

4. **Is the Offer Still Open for Acceptance**

     i. **Lapse:** an offer remains open only for a "reasonable time"

     j. **Has the Offer Been Revoked:**

       i. Revocation okay:
- Offeror can revoke an offer any time before it is accepted
- Offeror can revoke even if the offeror made a promise to keep it open — there is no consideration for the promise to keep it open
- Revocation is valid upon receipt. The revocation must be made before the acceptance — look to timing of the acceptance (Mailbox rule — see below in acceptance)

      ii.   Revocation not okay:
- Cannot revoke unilateral contract once the offeree started performance
- Cannot revoke if there is an option contract = consideration to hold open the offer; will be non-revocable during the time period agreed upon — even if one dies.
- Cannot revoke if the offer is a Firm Offer (2-205) (even if no consideration). Elements of a firm offer:
  - Offer was made by a merchant (reasonably expected to have knowledge or skill in that area)
  - To buy or sell goods
  - Signed writing by offeror
  - The signed writing gives assurance that it will be held open
  - If these elements are met, the offer is not revocable during the time stated or (if no time is stated) for a reasonable time; in no event may the period of irrevocability exceed 3 months

k.   **Rejection of offer:**
      i.   A counteroffer is a rejection of the initial offer (valid upon receipt of the rejection)

l.   **Destruction or Illegality:**
      i.   Destruction of subject matter of the contract (ex. the building gets destroyed by an earthquake)
      ii.   Subject matter of the contract becomes illegal

m. **Death:**
      i.   if one party dies, offer dies, except for option contracts

5.   Acceptance

n.   Elements of a valid acceptance:
      i.   A person must have knowledge of the offer
- *Robert v. Malm — must know about offer in order to accept it*

- government puts out reward for info on assault suspect; pl reported her assailer not
knowing about the open offer for a reward; the
court said she cannot collect the reward because a person must know about the offer in
order to accept it

ii. A person must intend to accept the offer
- Minority rule — the person performing has to
show that she intended to accept the offer;
burden is on the party performing
- Majority rule — performers actions alone creates a presumption that she did have the intent
to accept the offer

iii. Notice is sometimes required
- Bilateral contracts — need notice unless circumstances show otherwise
- Unilateral contracts — usually no notice needed unless circumstances show otherwise
- if the offeree has a reason to believe the offeror
has no means of learning of the acceptance,
the contract is void unless:
  - the offeree exercises reasonable diligence
to notify the offeror of the acceptance or
  - the offeror learns of the performance
within a reasonable time or
  - the offeror indicates that notification of
acceptance is not required
- *Carbolic Smoke case* — an ad for a device to
prevent the flu; the ad says the company will
pay money to anyone who purchases this device and ends up getting the flu; a person
bought it and still got the flu and wants his
money but company said he needed to first
give notice; the court said there was no requirement for the purchaser to give notice before he intended to perform; here valid acceptance was using the product and getting sick

o. **Who may accept the offer:**
  i. Only the person who the offer was directed towards
  ii. *Hypo* — if a person overhears an offer at Starbucks and accepts it, it is not valid

p. **How an offer can be accepted:** in "any reasonable manner"
  i. Performance one reasonable way unless offer says otherwise
  ii. If a party sends non-conforming goods, considered acceptance and breach unless says it is an accommodation.
  iii. Unreasonable method of acceptance: if there is no exclusive mode of acceptance, but the offeree transmits the acceptance by an unreasonable or unauthorized mode
    • Majority rule — MBR will not apply, and acceptance is effective when received
    • UCC rule — MBR will still apply even if the offeree dispatched the acceptance by an unreasonable method, as long as it is received by the offeror within the same time frame that it would have arrived if a reasonable mode had been used

q. **Timing of the Acceptance**
  i. General Rule — Acceptance is valid upon receipt
  ii. Exception — The Mailbox Rule (MBR):
    • An acceptance is valid once it is put in the mail if the acceptance was made with a method that is at least as efficient as the manner in which the offer was made.
    • Note: a rejection/revocation of an offer is effective upon actual receipt
    • When offeree reasonably dispatched an acceptance but is careless in addressing it
      - Majority rule — MBR will not apply, and acceptance is not effective until received by the offeror

- UCC rule — MBR will still apply if the acceptance is received by the offeror in the same time frame that it would have been received but for carelessly transmitting it

r. **An Acceptance with Different Terms**
  i. Common Law
     - Mirror Image Rule: If additional term is added, it is not an acceptance — it is considered a rejection unless "mirror image"
     - Last Shot Principle: last offer made before performance will make up the terms of the contract; the performance is the acceptance of the last offer; policy: meant to prevent clauses from slipping into the contract without one party realizing it
  ii. UCC 2-207: helps form contracts that are not mirror images, prevents last shot principle, and has a fallback in case there was a mess up
     - **2-207(1):** A definite and seasonable [timely] expression of acceptance or a written confirmation which is sent within a reasonable time operates as an acceptance even though it states terms additional to or different from those offered or agreed upon, *unless* acceptance is expressly made conditional on assent to the additional or different terms
     - **2-207(2):** Additional terms are construed as proposals for the contract (for non-merchants). However, b/w merchants, such additional terms become part of the contract unless:
        - The offer expressly limits acceptance to the terms of the offer; or
        - They materially alter it (ex. limited liability clause)
        - Notification of the objection to them has already been given or is given within a

reasonable time after notice of them is received

- **2-207(3):** If no contract, you still might have a
  contract formed based on the conduct of the
  parties; terms of the contract will only consist
  to those that are matching (different terms
  will be knocked out)

Sample Condensed Outline
Contract Formation

What law applies to contracts?

UCC: sale of goods (moveable items)
Common Law: services or real estate
Mixed between goods and services: predominant purpose

Is a Contract Formed?
1. Mutual Assent
    a. Must be meeting of the minds
    b. Look to the offers and acceptance
    c. Measure using an objectively reasonable person standard
2. Consideration
    a. Bargained for exchange —
        i.   the Promisee must suffer a legal detriment
        ii. the detriment must induce the promise
        iii. the promise must induce the detriment
    b. Amount of consideration does not matter: don't need equivalence between what is promised and what the detriment is
    c. No consideration for gifts. past consideration, illusory promises, output/requirement contracts, pre-existing duty rule
3. Offer
    a. Must be directed towards a specific person
    b. Ads are not offer, but rather an invitation to negotiate
    c. Look for definitive terms and/or promissory words
    d. Look to whether the offer was made in jest/joke
4. Is the Offer Still Open for Acceptance?
    a. **Lapse:** an offer remains open only for a "reasonable time"
    b. **Has the Offer Been Revoked?**
        i. Revocation okay:
            • any time before it is accepted

- even if the offeror made a promise to keep it open
- valid upon receipt

    ii.   Revocation not okay:
- once the offeree started performance
- if there is an option contract
- if the offer is a Firm Offer (2-205); *Elements*:
    - Offer was made by a merchant
    - To buy or sell goods
    - In a signed writing by offeror
    - The signed writing gives assurance that it will be held open
    - (if these elements, no revocable for time stated/reasonable time/can't exceed 3 months)

  c. **Rejection of offer?**
    i.   A counteroffer is a rejection of the initial offer (valid upon receipt)

  d. **Destruction or Illegality?**
    i.   Destruction of subject matter terminates offer
    ii. Subject matter becomes illegal terminates offer

  e. **Death?**
    i.   if one party dies, offer dies, except for option contracts

5.   **Acceptance**
  a. **Elements of an Acceptance**
    i.   Must have knowledge of the offer
    ii. Must intend to accept the offer
    iii. Notice is required in bilateral contracts, but usually not for unilateral contracts

  b. **Who may accept the offer?**
    i.   only the person who the offer was directed towards

  c. **How an offer can be accepted: in "any reasonable manner"**
    i.   Performance one reasonable way unless offer says otherwise

      ii.   If a party sends non-conforming goods, considered breach unless says it is an accommodation.

      iii. Unreasonable method of acceptance?

- Majority rule—no MBR; acceptance not effective until received
- UCC rule—MBR will still apply as long as received by the offeror within the same time frame

d. **Timing of the Acceptance**

      i.   General Rule—Acceptance is valid upon receipt

- Exception—The Mailbox Rule (MBR):
  - acceptance is valid once it is put in the mail
  - a rejection/revocation of an offer is effective upon actual receipt
- Careless in addressing acceptance?
  - Majority rule—no MBR; acceptance not effective until received
  - UCC rule—MBR will still apply as long as received in the same time frame

e. **An Acceptance with Different Terms**

      i.   Common Law

- Mirror Image Rule: If additional terms are added, considered a rejection; must be mirror image
- Last Shot Principle: prevent clauses from slipping into the contract

      ii. UCC 2-207:

- 2-207(1): Timely acceptance sent within a reasonable time operates as an acceptance even though it states additional terms, *unless* acceptance is expressly made conditional on assent to the additional terms
- 2-207(2):
  - **for non-merchants:** additional terms are proposals

- **for merchants:** additional terms are part of the contract unless:
  - · offer expressly limits acceptance to the terms of the offer; or
  - · materially alter it
  - · notification of the objection to them has already been given
- **2-207(3):** can still have a contract formed based on the conduct of the parties
  - terms will only consist to those that are matching, and different terms will be knocked out

Sample Flow Cart

Here is a sample flow chart for one the topics in the previous contracts formation outline.

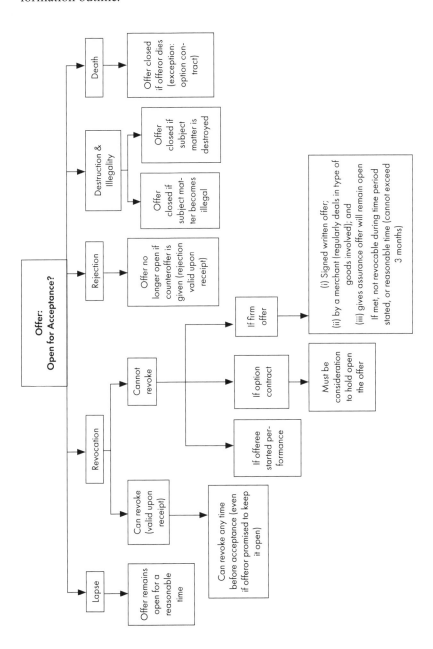

SAMPLE FINAL EXAM

Sample Exam Question

CIVIL PROCEDURE ESSAY
(Suggested Time: 75 min.)

In October 2009, while visiting New York, Pam and her sister were injured when their car collided with Abe's car after Abe ran a red light. Pam, who was her sister's passenger, suffered significant pain in her neck, including bruising and swelling. Pam did not see a doctor. A week later, after Pam returned to California, Pam was in another car collision. This time the accident was between Pam and Bella. The collision occurred because Bella was speeding and talking on her cell phone. After the accident, Pam was diagnosed with a hairline cervical fracture (i.e., a minor break of a neck bone). The doctor was unable to determine whether the first or second car accident caused the fracture.

Pam and her sister sued Abe and Bella in one action. Pam asserted negligence claims seeking $100,000 from each defendant. Pam's sister asserted a negligence claim against Abe for $75,000. Pam and her sister filed the suit in a California federal court. Pam alleged in her complaint that both accidents caused her neck injury. Pam and her sister are California citizens, while Abe and Bella are New York citizens. Abe has never been to California. He has no friends or family there. He has never done any business in California and does not own property there.

Abe intended to take a week vacation in Seattle starting on December 1, 2009, so Abe booked a direct, non-stop flight from New York to Seattle. A month before the flight, the airline notified Abe by email that the flight would no longer be direct: the plane would land in San Francisco before continuing on to Seattle. Abe never saw the email, however, and did not learn of the stop until after the flight left New York. Pam, however, learned that Abe would be landing in San Francisco and hired a process server. The plane landed in San Francisco and the process server boarded the plane (he had bought a ticket for the flight from San Francisco to Seattle). While the plane was still grounded in California, the process server served Abe with the summons and complaint.

Abe filed three motions to dismiss with the court. Abe's first motion contended that under the Federal Rules of Civil Procedure Abe and Bella may not be joined as co-defendants in the same lawsuit. He further argued that the claims against him should be dismissed for misjoinder. Abe's second motion asserted that the court did not have subject matter jurisdiction over the sister's claim against Abe. Abe's third motion asserted that the court did not have personal jurisdiction over him. The court denied all three of Abe's motions.

Please answer the following three questions:

1. Did the court correctly decline to dismiss the claims against Abe and find that he and Bella were properly joined as co-defendants? (35 points)

2. Did the court correctly find it had subject matter jurisdiction over the sister's claim against Abe? Federal question jurisdiction does not exist for any claim in the lawsuit and you should not discuss that basis for jurisdiction. (25 points)

3. Did the court correctly find it had personal jurisdiction over Abe? (40 points)

Sample Exam Answer

CIVIL PROCEDURE ESSAY EXAM
Sample Essay Exam Answer

1. Did the court correctly decline the motion to dismiss and find that Abe and Bella were properly joined as co-defendants?

Joinder

Parties may be sued as co-defendants if two requirements are met. First, the asserted right to relief must arise from the same transaction and occurrence or series of transactions or occurrences. Second, a question of law or fact common to both defendants must exist.

i. Same Transaction or Occurrence

In determining whether claims arise from the same transaction or occurrence or series of transactions or occurrences, courts often apply the logical relation test. Claims are logically related if separate trials on each of the claims would involve a substantial duplication of effort and time by the parties and the courts. Courts have tended to interpret this rule broadly. Courts are often flexible, making a common-sense assessment as to whether joinder in a single case is fair. Some courts have found that when an injury has two causes and the harm attributable to each cause is indeterminable, that it is appropriate to view the same transaction requirement as satisfied.

Here, Abe could argue the accidents are not logically related because they occurred at different times (a week apart), in different places (New York versus California), and involved different people (Abe versus Bella). In the first accident, Pam was not driving, but was just a passenger in her sister's car. The second accident involved a different driver (Pam) in a different car. The causes of the accidents were also different (speeding/talking on phone versus running a red light). The witnesses in each case (such as any emergency responders, police, fire, etc., and any bystanders) would also be different as the accidents occurred a week apart and in different parts of the country. Thus, trying the claims separately would not involve a substantial disruption of effort and time by the parties or the court because there are so many different pieces of evidence to introduce for each case. Furthermore, the accidents occurred in different states; thus the substantive law and choice of law rules may also be different, which has the potential to confuse the jury if the case was heard together.

On the other hand, Pam could argue that because courts have tended to interpret the logical relation test broadly, a court may find the two claims can be joined. Here, a series of occurrences — the two accidents — caused Pam's injury. The injury in both claims is the same (i.e., the broken neck). Thus, the evidence related to damages and causation will be the same in both claims. Trying the claims separately will cause substantial effort and time by the parties and the court because the same evidence would be introduced twice. Furthermore, Pam's claims involve an injury with two causes and the harm attributable to each cause is indeterminable because the doctor was unable to determine whether the first or second car accident caused the fracture in Pam's neck. Thus, the injury is not clearly attributable to one accident or the other, which is one reason given by the courts to view the same transaction requirement as satisfied.

In addition, a strong policy consideration exists for hearing both claims together. Should the cases not be heard together the plaintiff may be "whipsawed." A whipsawed plaintiff may well convince two juries that she is entitled to recovery, but end up with nothing, since each jury believed the absent defendant was the responsible party. If the claims are tried separately, each defendant may point fingers at the other defendant and claim the absent party caused the injury. The result could be that the innocent plaintiff recovers from neither defendant. Finally, the claims are fairly straightforward negligence claims from a simple event (a car accident) — so a jury should be easily able to understand the key issues if the two claims are combined. Given the congestion in the courts and the desire to reduce litigation, a court is likely to err on the side of permitting claims to be joined when doing so would be efficient.

Given the possible unfairness of allowing a plaintiff to be whipsawed, the desire for efficiency and the reduction of multiplicity of actions, as well as the flexibility underlying the rules, a court is likely to find the claims arose from the same transaction or occurrence.

ii. Common Question of Law or Fact

To be legally joined, a question of common law or fact between two claims must exist. The requirement that claims involve common questions or law or fact usually does not present a difficulty when claims are transactionally related.

Here, several questions common to both lawsuits exist, including the cause of the neck injury and the extent of Pam's injuries/damages. There might also be common issues surrounding any alleged contributory negligence on Pam's part.

Therefore, there are common questions of law and fact and this element is satisfied.

Dismissal by Misjoinder

Misjoinder is not a basis for dismissing an action. The remedy for misjoinder is to sever. (Rule 21). Severance results in two separate suits, each with its own docket number and judgment.

Here, Abe sought dismissal for misjoinder — exactly what Rule 21 prohibits.

Therefore, even if Abe and Bella were not properly joined, the court was correct in denying the motion to dismiss.

2. Did the court correctly find it had subject matter jurisdiction over the sister's claim against Abe?

Federal courts are courts of limited jurisdiction. If a court does not have original jurisdiction, it must have supplemental jurisdiction to hear the claim. Here, the question says federal question jurisdiction does not exist. Thus, there must be either diversity jurisdiction or supplemental jurisdiction.

Diversity Jurisdiction

For a court to have diversity jurisdiction two requirements must be satisfied: (1) complete diversity of citizenship exists (i.e., that the plaintiffs and defendants are citizens of different states); and (2) the amount in controversy exceeds $75,000. With respect to the second element, multiple plaintiffs may not aggregate separate and distinct claims. The only exception is if the plaintiffs hold a common and undivided interest (e.g., ownership of a common fund or partnership).

Complete diversity of citizenship exists because the facts state that the sister is a California citizen and Abe is a New York citizen. However, the second element — the amount in controversy — is not met. The sister is suing for exactly $75,000, and therefore the statutory requirement that the dispute be for *more* than $75,000 has not been met. Because the complaint is for less than the required amount, the defendant can establish to a legal certainty that plaintiff failed to meet the amount-in-controversy requirement.

The sister cannot meet the amount in controversy requirement by aggregating her claim with Pam's claim. In this case, there is no common and undivided interest because the damages are easily separated. Pam's injury is to her neck, while her sister is not seeking recovery for Pam's injured neck but presumably her own injuries and the damage to her car. There is also no common and undivided interest because the claims have been separated (P seeks $100,000, while the sister seeks $75,000). No facts are given that would suggest somehow the claims of Pam and her sister are the same.

Because the amount in controversy has not been met, diversity jurisdiction does not exist over the sister's claim.

Supplemental Jurisdiction

Even if the court lacks original jurisdiction over all claims, it will be able to hear the jurisdictionally insufficient claim if supplemental jurisdiction exists. A court may have supplemental jurisdiction over closely related claims (1367(a)), so long as the claim is not by a plaintiff against a party joined under FRCP Rules 14, 19, 20 or 24 (1367(b)).

i. 1367(a) — Relatedness Analysis

Claims are sufficiently related to form one case or controversy under Article III if they arise from a common nucleus of operative facts. (1367(a) and *Gibbs*).

Here, Pam and her sister's claims arise from a common nucleus of operative facts because both Pam and her sister were injured in a car accident with Abe. They were in the same car together when the accident occurred and were injured at the same time. Pam's and her sister's injuries arise from the same event — Abe running a red light.

Therefore the court will find the claims are sufficiently related to form one case or controversy.

ii. 1367(b) — Supplemental Analysis in Diversity Cases

The court is barred from exercising supplemental jurisdiction, however, under 1367(b). When the basis for original jurisdiction is in diversity, supplemental jurisdiction does not exist if the claim is: (1) by a plaintiff; and (2) against a part joined under Rules 14, 19. 20 or 24.

Here, the court may not exercise supplemental jurisdiction. First, Pam's claim against Abe (the anchor claim) sounds in diversity. The facts say there exists no federal question jurisdiction, that Pam and Abe are citizens of different states (California v. New York) and that the amount in controversy is over $75,000 (Pam is suing for $100,000). Second, this is a claim by a plaintiff. The facts tell us that the sister is a plaintiff suing Abe. Third, this is a claim against a party joined under Rule 20. The facts say that the sister is suing Abe, and the analysis from question #1 above shows that Abe and Bella are joined under Rule 20 as co-defendants.

The requirements of 1367(a)(2) carve-out are met, and the court thus does not have supplemental jurisdiction over this claim. The court was probably mistaken in not granting Abe's second motion to dismiss.

3. Did the court correctly find it had personal jurisdiction over Abe? (40 points)

Both a statutory and a constitutional analysis is required to determine whether a court has personal jurisdiction.

<u>Long Arm Statute Analysis</u>

In a federal court, jurisdiction is limited by FRCP Rule 4(k). That rules say that federal courts must apply the long-arm of the state in which the federal court sits.

Here the case is pending before a California federal court. The California long-arm statute extends California court's jurisdiction to the fullest extent permitted under the U.S. Constitution.

Therefore, if the exercise of jurisdiction is constitutional, the long-arm requirements are also met.

<u>The Constitutional Analysis</u>

The 14th Amendment's Due Process Clause limits a court's authority to enter judgments against defendants who has insufficient connections to the forum in which the court sits. If a party is personally served while physically present within the forum state, the issue is whether tag jurisdiction exists (under *Burnham*). The Supreme Court has been unclear, however, as to the basis for tag jurisdiction and courts have taken two analytical approaches.

i. A Territorial Theory of Jurisdiction (Scalia)

Under one approach (set forth by Scalia in *Burnham*), jurisdiction exists when a defendant is physically present in the state and is personally served. Under this territorial theory of jurisdiction, the basis for jurisdiction lies in the English tradition and American common law — dating before the landmark *Pennoyer* case — which found that every state may rightfully exercise jurisdiction over persons within its territory. While cases like *International Shoe* (and later *Shaffer v. Heitner*) meant that states would not be bound to adhere to the unbending territorial limits set forth in *Pennoyer*, transitory presence remains a basis of jurisdiction consistent with the due process standard. Under this analytical approach, jurisdiction based on physical presence alone does not violate due process and therefore need not be subjected to the International Shoe minimum contacts analysis. Cases have found that jurisdiction is proper even when the defendant is in the state involuntarily. See, e.g., *People v. Williams* (personal jurisdiction over person involuntarily confined to state hospital).

If the court adopts the territorial theory of jurisdiction, the facts say that Abe was personally served when in San Francisco. Because Abe was served while in California, jurisdiction is established. The fact that Abe was in the state for a brief period of time is irrelevant: personal service upon a physically present defendant suffices to confer jurisdiction regardless of whether the defendant is only briefly in the state. Nor is it relevant under a territorial theory whether the defendant was in the state voluntarily. Under a territorial theory — the mere presence alone is sufficient. Even if voluntariness was an issue, no facts exist to suggest that Abe was forced into the state or entered in voluntarily (in the sense of being tricked).

Thus, under the territorial theory, the court would have personal jurisdiction over Abe.

ii. A Modern Approach (Brennan)

But courts have also applied a second analytical approach to tag jurisdiction (set forth by Brennan in *Burnham*). Under this second approach, all forms of jurisdiction must comport with modern notions of due process. Although in-state service will often meet these requirements, a categorical rule does not exist. This is particularly true when a defendant is present in a forum involuntarily. When the defendant is in the state for a particularly brief period of time this also suggests that the exercise of jurisdiction may be unreasonable.

Under this approach, it's unlikely that jurisdiction should exist. Jurisdiction under the modern approach exists only if the defendant has minimum contacts with the forum. Minimum contacts can consist of either (i) isolated or occasional contacts purposefully directed toward the form (specific jurisdiction) or (ii) systematic and continuous contact with the form (general jurisdiction). Furthermore, the minimum contacts must be sufficient such that the exercise of jurisdiction comports with traditional notions of fair play and substantial justice.

a. Specific Jurisdiction

Specific jurisdiction exists over claims that arise from a defendant's forum activity, so long as the defendant has purposefully availed itself of the privileges and benefits of the forum state.

Specific jurisdiction will not exist because Abe's landing in San Francisco (his contact with California) did not give rise to the lawsuit (i.e., the accident, which occurred a month earlier in NY). Nor did Abe purposefully avail himself of the benefits of California, since he did not reach out and deliberately get involved in a car accident with a California citizen. He did not intend or plan to be in California at all: the facts say he did not realize he was going to land in California until after he boarded the plan.

Thus, specific jurisdiction does not exist.

b. General Jurisdiction

General jurisdiction exists when a defendant has continuous, systematic and substantial contacts with a state.

Abe does not have continuous, systematic or substantial contacts with California because the facts say that Abe has never been to California, has no family or friends there, has never done business in California, and does not own property there.

Thus, general jurisdiction also does not exist.

c. Traditional Notions of Fair Play and Substantial Justice

Even if the defendant has minimum contacts with the forum, the jurisdiction over defendant must comport with notional of fair play and substantial justice.

The exercise of jurisdiction over Abe would be unreasonable (not comporting with traditional notions of fair play and substantial justice) given the short period of time Abe spent in the state, the lack of any attempt to use California services, the fortuity of service on Abe and the hardship of him having to travel to defend in California. In *Burnham* jurisdiction was found on very slim connections, but the connections here are slimmer still.

Thus, using the modern approach, personal jurisdiction over Abe is unlikely.

iii. Reconciliation between Territorial Theory and Modern Approach

It is unclear which approach the court should apply. On the one hand, the territorial approach that Scalia has described might lead to greater predictability, efficiency, and consistency. It creates a bright-line rule that is easy to apply and reduces judicial discretion and ad hoc decisions. Predictability in procedure is important because it allows defendants to conform their behavior. Also the U.S. Supreme Court has turned more conservative in recent years, and Scalia's historical approach may be attractive to other members of the Court.

On the other hand, the territorial approach, like any categorical rule, can be wooden and lead to unfair results in some cases. In this particular case, the territorial approach seems to unnecessarily burden Abe with fortuitous assertions of jurisdiction. Certainly jurisdiction in this context seems inconsistent with the idea that jurisdiction should limit a court's power to hear cases involving defendants with little connections to the forum, or that a defendant must have done something "purposefully" to have a connection with the forum. Tag jurisdiction for transient defendants is also inconsistent with the approach used in many other countries and some commentators have argued violates international law. Lastly, the territorial approach is very hard to reconcile with the court's earlier decisions in *Shaffer* and *International Shoe*.

The courts have been split in which approach they take. On balance, however, given that the car accident occurred in New York and the witnesses and evidence is there, and because Abe did not intend to visit California and was served only fortuitously, jurisdiction seems unlikely.

SAMPLE OBJECTIVE MEMORANDA

In Chapter 7, you learned the basics of writing an objective memorandum. Part of your lesson included how to organize your arguments in an objective memorandum. You learned to include initial arguments first, followed by counter-arguments, followed by rebuttal arguments. Although most professors use this traditional approach, some professors prefer an alternative organization. The alternative organization eliminates the rebuttal and merges all arguments into two categories: "Winning Arguments" and "Losing Arguments." Under this alternative approach, the writer sets forth the arguments that are less likely to prevail first (the "Losing Arguments"), followed by the arguments that are more likely to prevail (the "Winning Arguments").

This Appendix includes an example of each approach. The first example memorandum illustrates the traditional "Initial Argument — Counter-Argument — Rebuttal Argument" approach. The second example memorandum illustrates the alternative "Losing Arguments — Winning Arguments" approach.

A. Example Memorandum with Traditional Organization

MEMORANDUM

To: Partner
From: Associate
Re: Sophie Burns; Search of Visitor's Belongings

I. Question Presented

Under the Fourth Amendment, which prohibits search and seizure of an individual's belongings without a warrant, was Sophie Burns' backpack lawfully searched pursuant to a premises warrant when (i) she was a visitor to the premises and stopped by her friends' apartment to take a shower and drink a few beers before attending a football game; (ii) her backpack was at the front door next to a pair of men's shoes, but the backpack was marked with the emblem "H" and the word "Crimson;" and (iii) Sophie was wearing a Harvard t-shirt while the male occupants of the premises were both wearing Boston University insignia?

II. Brief Answer

No, Sophie Burns' backpack was likely not lawfully searched. The search of a visitor's belongings is permissible only if (i) the container searched belonged to someone who had a relationship with the premises of more than a "mere passerby;" or (ii) the officer conducting the search lacks notice that the belongings were owned by the visitor. Here, the search of Sophie's backpack was unlawful for two reasons. First, Sophie did not have a relationship with the premises because she was merely passing by on her way to a college football game and stopped at the apartment for a quick shower and a few beers. Although she took a shower at the apartment, her visit was temporary and she was not involved in any unusual activity on the premises. Second, the officers conducting the search had constructive notice that the Harvard backpack belonged to Sophie. Although the backpack was next to a pair of men's shoes, it was marked with the Harvard insignia "H," the word "Crimson," and was the same colors associated with Harvard

College. Sophie was wearing a Harvard t-shirt. Both male occupants of the property were wearing Boston University insignia. Thus, the search of Sophie's backpack was unlawful.

III. Statement of Facts

This firm represents Sophie Burns, a Harvard college student, who was recently charged with possession of narcotics. Sophie was visiting her friends Daniel and Anton at their apartment in Cambridge at the time officers executed a warrant to search Daniel and Anton's apartment for stolen merchandise. As part of the search, one of the officers, Officer Braxton, searched Sophie's backpack and found narcotics.

Sophie has known Daniel and Anton for three years and frequently stops by their apartment prior to Harvard football games to say hello and drink a few beers because their apartment is within close proximity of the stadium. On this particular occasion, Sophie decided to shower and get ready for the football game at Daniel and Anton's apartment. She had never done this before, but she was coming straight from work and did not want to go out of her way to go home to shower. Daniel and Anton suggested that she get ready at their apartment. After arriving at the apartment, Sophie dropped her backpack at the front door next to a pair of size twelve men's shoes. Her backpack was red, black, and grey. It had the symbol "H," and had the words "Crimson" written across the front. Sophie proceeded to take a shower. After her shower, she got dressed and stretched out on the couch as she drank a beer. She was wearing a red Harvard t-shirt, jeans, her hair was wet, and she was barefoot. She had a Harvard hat next to her on the couch.

Within minutes of Sophie relaxing on the couch, two police officers knocked on the door with a warrant to search the premises. The warrant stated two male occupants lived at the apartment. When the officers entered the apartment, Sophie was lying on the couch. Daniel was sitting on a chair next to her and was wearing jeans and a Boston University sweatshirt. Anton was wearing jeans, a dress shirt, and had on a hat that said "BU." The police officers searched the entire premises. Before leaving, one of the police officers, Officer Braxton, picked up Sophie's backpack at the front door and looked inside. No one said anything to Officer Braxton during the search. Officer Braxton found narcotics in the backpack. Sophie was charged with the unlawful possession of narcotics.

IV. Discussion

Conclusion

    Sophie's belongings were likely searched unlawfully. A valid warrant must describe the "place to be searched, and the persons or things to be seized." *United States v. Mousli*, 511 F.3d 7, 12 (1st Cir. 2007). When executing a search warrant, officers are permitted to search all containers within the premises that could conceal the type of property listed in the warrant. *United States v. Gray*, 814 F.2d 49, 51 (1st Cir. 1987). However, a visitor's belongings are generally excluded from the search. *Id.* The search of a visitor's belongings is only permissible if (i) the visitor has a relationship with the premises; or (ii) the officer conducting the search lacks notice that the belongings were owned by a visitor. *Id.*

Rule Paragraph

    A visitor's belongings may be lawfully searched if the visitor has a relationship with the premises. *Id.* A visitor has a relationship with the premises if the visitor is present during criminal activity or if the visitor's presence is more than temporary. *Id.* In *Gray*, officers searched the jacket of a visitor while executing a search warrant for the premises. *Id.* at 50. The visitor was at the premises at 3:45 a.m. after "a drug deal had just gone down." *Id.* The court held the visitor's belongings were lawfully searched because there was a "relationship between the person and the place." *Id.* at 51. The court explained the visitor was not "a casual afternoon visitor to the premises," but was at the premises at an "unusual hour" during criminal activity. *Id.* The circumstances thus suggested he was more than a "mere visitor or passerby." *Id.*; *see also United States v. Giwa*, 831 F.2d 538, 545 (5th Cir. 1986) (holding a defendant's belongings were lawfully searched because he was an overnight guest, alone on the premises, and answered the door "clad only in a bathrobe and slacks," suggesting he had "more than just a temporary presence in the apartment").

Explanation Paragraph #1

Explanation Paragraph #2

    A visitor's belongings may also be searched if the officer conducting the search lacks notice that the belongings were owned by the visitor. *Id.* The location of the belongings and markings on the belongings can provide constructive notice that an item belongs to a visitor. *Id.* In *Gray*, the officers searched a visitor's red, nylon jacket. *Id.* at 50. The jacket was draped over the back of a chair in an "outer room." *Id.* The court held that the officers' search of the jacket was lawful because the officers had no reason to know it belonged to a visitor. *Id.* at 51. The court explained that the jacket was not found as "part of a group of personal effects identified with a particular individual." *Id.* Furthermore, the jacket "was bereft of any external indicia of ownership — there was no lettering, nametag, or the like to alert the searchers." *Id.* The jacket "could have been designed for a man or a woman or without regard to gender." *Id.* The officers thus "did not know — nor did the circumstances prompt them to inquire — who owned the jackets found in the entry room." *Id.*

Sophie's backpack was likely not lawfully searched. First, Sophie was a mere passerby and had no relationship to the premises. Unlike the visitor in *Gray,* who was found at the premises at 3:45 a.m. in the middle of a drug bust, Sophie was merely visiting friends in the afternoon before a football game. There was nothing unusual about her visit and the officers had no reason to believe she was involved in any criminal wrongdoing. Sophie was simply stopping by the apartment to take a shower and have a few beers before heading to a football game. She planned to stay for a short time and nothing about her circumstances suggested she was more than a casual visitor who planned a temporary visit to see her friends.

Application: Initial Arguments: Point #1

Furthermore, a court will likely find Officer Braxton was put on notice that the backpack belonged to Sophie. Unlike the red nylon jacket in *Gray,* which could have belonged to anyone in the apartment, the Crimson backpack was tied directly to Sophie. The backpack had the Harvard emblem "H" on the front and the word "Crimson." It was the colors of Harvard College: red, black, and grey. Sophie was wearing a Harvard t-shirt. No one else in the apartment had any Harvard insignia on their clothing or in their possession. In fact, the two occupants of the apartment who were subject

Application: Initial Arguments: Point #2

to the warrant both had on Boston University insignia, suggesting the backpack did not belong to them. Thus, Officer Braxton should have known the backpack belonged to Sophie, a visitor.

The prosecution will argue that the search Sophie's backpack was lawful. First, the prosecution can argue that Sophie had a relationship with the premises. Just as spending the night and answering the door in a robe in *Giwa* suggested more than a mere temporary presence, Sophie's actions of taking a shower and getting dressed at the apartment suggest more than a mere temporary presence at the apartment. Sophie felt so comfortable at the apartment that she chose to shower and dress there in lieu of her own home. At the time the officers arrived, she was stretched out on the couch, with wet hair, and her shoes off. Sophie was so comfortable with the apartment that she engaged in activities typically done only by occupants of a home. Thus, Sophie was not merely "passing by" or a "casual visitor" to the apartment. She had a relationship with the premises.

Second, the prosecution can argue Officer Braxton did not have notice that the backpack belonged to Sophie. Like the nylon jacket in *Gray*, which was located in an "outer room," Sophie's backpack was located in an "outer room." It was at the front door. In fact, it was next to a pair of men's shoes, indicating it belonged to one of the two male occupants listed on the search warrant. Furthermore, just as the nylon jacket in *Gray* had no lettering or nametag to alert the officers about the jacket's ownership, Sophie's backpack had no lettering or name tag to alert Officer Braxton that the backpack belonged to Sophie. Sophie's backpack had an "H" and said "Crimson;" however, neither of these markings suggest the backpack belonged to Sophie rather than one of the male occupants. Although Sophie had on a Harvard t-shirt, the backpack did not say "Harvard." The connection between an "H" and "Harvard" is too remote to expect Officer Braxton to know they were the same. The backpack was just like the red nylon jacket in *Gray*, which could have

Application:
Counter-
Arguments:
Point #1

Application:
Counter-
Arguments:
Point #2

equally belonged to anyone at the apartment. Thus, the circumstances did not give Officer Braxton adequate notice that the backpack belonged to Sophie.

The prosecution's arguments are likely to fail. First, the prosecution's argument that Sophie had a relationship with the premises will likely fail. Sophie's decision to shower at the premises and drink a few beers does not take away her constitutional right to be free from unlawful search and seizure. The defendant's decision in *Giwa* to spend the night at the premises alone, without the occupants present, made his relationship with the premises more like that of an occupant. Here, Sophie did not spend the night at the apartment and was not alone in the apartment. Merely sitting on a couch to have a beer at her friends' apartment prior to attending a football game does not equate her to an occupant. Further, showering does not equate one to the status of an occupant. It is common for a visitor, especially a college student, to take a quick shower at a friend's place right before going out. Sophie was simply in a hurry and only planned to stay at the apartment temporarily before heading to the game. Thus, Sophie's circumstances suggest her stay was temporary and she was nothing more than a mere passerby.

> **Application:** Rebuttal Arguments: Point #1

Second, the prosecution's argument that Officer Braxton lacked notice will likely fail. The location of Sophie's backpack near the front door indicated it belonged to a visitor. Occupants do not typically leave their backpacks at the front door, but are more likely to bring belongings into a bedroom or to a kitchen table. Visitors, on the other hand, are more likely to drop a backpack at the door as they walk in. Thus, the location of the backpack indicated it could belong to Sophie. Furthermore, although the backpack was sitting next to a pair of men's shoes, the markings on the backpack indicated it belonged to Sophie and not one of the male occupants. The connection between the letter "H" with the word "Crimson" next to it and Harvard College is not remote. Most residents of Cambridge, where the search took place, are familiar with the Harvard "H" and the Harvard colors.

> **Application:** Rebuttal Arguments: Point #2

The apartment was also in close proximity to Harvard College, so officers who work in the area would know the "H" emblem stood for "Harvard." Given the location of the backpack near the door, the colors on the backpack, and the insignia inscribed on it, Officer Braxton should have at least inquired as to who owned the backpack. As Officer Braxton had sufficient notice that the backpack belonged to Sophie, he was not legally permitted to search it.

Conclusion
Therefore, a court will likely find the officer's search of Sophie's backpack was unlawful.

V. Conclusion

A court will likely find that Sophie's backpack was unlawfully searched. Sophie was a mere visitor to the apartment who was passing by on the way to a football game and had no relationship to the premises. Furthermore, Officer Braxton was put on notice that the backpack belonged to Sophie because it had Harvard insignia and Sophie was the only one in the apartment wearing a Harvard t-shirt. Thus, the search was likely unlawful.

B. Example Memorandum with Alternative Organization

MEMORANDUM

To: Partner
From: Associate
Re: Sophie Burns; Search of Visitor's Belongings

I. Question Presented

Under the Fourth Amendment, which prohibits search and seizure of an individual's belongings without a warrant, was Sophie Burns' backpack lawfully searched pursuant to a premises warrant when (i) she was a visitor to the premises and stopped by her friends' apartment to take a shower and drink a few beers before attending a football game; (ii) her backpack was at the front door next to a pair of men's shoes, but the backpack was marked with the emblem "H" and the word "Crimson;" and (iii) Sophie was wearing a Harvard t-shirt while the male occupants of the premises were both wearing Boston University insignia?

II. Brief Answer

No, Sophie Burns' backpack was likely not lawfully searched. The search of a visitor's belongings is permissible only if (i) the container searched belonged to someone who had a relationship with the premises of more than a "mere passerby;" or (ii) the officer conducting the search lacks notice that the belongings were owned by the visitor. Here, the search of Sophie's backpack was unlawful for two reasons. First, Sophie did not have a relationship with the premises because she was merely passing by on her way to a college football game and stopped at the apartment for a quick shower and a few beers. Although she took a shower at the apartment, her visit was temporary and she was not involved in any unusual activity on the premises. Second, the officers conducting the search had constructive notice that the Harvard backpack belonged to Sophie. Although the backpack was next to a pair of men's shoes, it was marked with the Harvard insignia "H," the word "Crimson," and was the same colors associated with Harvard

College. Sophie was wearing a Harvard t-shirt. Both male occupants of the property were wearing Boston University insignia. Thus, the search of Sophie's backpack was unlawful.

III. Statement of Facts

This firm represents Sophie Burns, a Harvard college student, who was recently charged with possession of narcotics. Sophie was visiting her friends Daniel and Anton at their apartment in Cambridge at the time officers executed a warrant to search Daniel and Anton's apartment for stolen merchandise. As part of the search, one of the officers, Officer Braxton, searched Sophie's backpack and found narcotics.

Sophie has known Daniel and Anton for three years and frequently stops by their apartment prior to Harvard football games to say hello and drink a few beers because their apartment is within close proximity of the stadium. On this particular occasion, Sophie decided to shower and get ready for the football game at Daniel and Anton's apartment. She had never done this before, but she was coming straight from work and did not want to go out of her way to go home to shower. Daniel and Anton suggested that she get ready at their apartment. After arriving at the apartment, Sophie dropped her backpack at the front door next to a pair of size twelve men's shoes. Her backpack was red, black, and grey. It had the symbol "H," and had the words "Crimson" written across the front. Sophie proceeded to take a shower. After her shower, she got dressed and stretched out on the couch as she drank a beer. She was wearing a red Harvard t-shirt, jeans, her hair was wet, and she was barefoot. She had a Harvard hat next to her on the couch.

Within minutes of Sophie relaxing on the couch, two police officers knocked on the door with a warrant to search the premises. The warrant stated two male occupants lived at the apartment. When the officers entered the apartment, Sophie was lying on the couch. Daniel was sitting on a chair next to her and was wearing jeans and a Boston University sweatshirt. Anton was wearing jeans, a dress shirt, and had on a hat that said "BU." The police officers searched the entire premises. Before leaving, one of the police officers, Officer Braxton, picked up Sophie's backpack at the front door and looked inside. No one said anything to Officer Braxton during the search. Officer Braxton found narcotics in the backpack. Sophie was charged with the unlawful possession of narcotics.

IV. Discussion

Sophie's belongings were likely searched unlawfully. A valid warrant must describe the "place to be searched, and the persons or things to be seized." *United States v. Mousli*, 511 F.3d 7, 12 (1st Cir. 2007). When executing a search warrant, officers are permitted to search all containers within the premises that could conceal the type of property listed in the warrant. *United States v. Gray*, 814 F.2d 49, 51 (1st Cir. 1987). However, a visitor's belongings are generally excluded from the search. *Id.* The search of a visitor's belongings is only permissible if (i) the visitor has a relationship with the premises; or (ii) the officer conducting the search lacks notice that the belongings were owned by a visitor. *Id.*

A visitor's belongings may be lawfully searched if the visitor has a relationship to the premises. *Id.* A visitor has a relationship with the premises if the visitor is present during criminal activity or if the visitor's presence is more than temporary. *Id.* In *Gray*, officers searched the jacket of a visitor while executing a search warrant for the premises. *Id.* at 50. The visitor was at the premises at 3:45 a.m. after "a drug deal had just gone down." *Id.* The court held the visitor's belongings were lawfully searched because there was a "relationship between the person and the place." *Id.* at 51. The court explained the visitor was not "a casual afternoon visitor to the premises," but was at the premises at an "unusual hour" during criminal activity. *Id.* The circumstances thus suggested he was more than a "mere visitor or passerby." *Id.*; *see also United States v. Giwa*, 831 F.2d 538, 545 (5th Cir. 1986) (holding a defendant's belongings were lawfully searched because he was an overnight guest, alone on the premises, and answered the door "clad only in a bathrobe and slacks," suggesting he had "more than just a temporary presence in the apartment").

A visitor's belongings may also be searched if the officer conducting the search lacks notice that the belongings were owned by the visitor. *Id.* The location of the belongings and markings on the belongings can provide constructive notice

Conclusion

Rule Paragraph

Explanation Paragraph #1

Explanation Paragraph #2

that an item belongs to a visitor. *Id.* In *Gray*, the officers searched a visitor's red, nylon jacket. *Id.* at 50. The jacket was draped over the back of a chair in an "outer room." *Id.* The court held that the officers' search of the jacket was lawful because the officers had no reason to know it belonged to a visitor. *Id.* at 51. The court explained that the jacket was not found as "part of a group of personal effects identified with a particular individual." *Id.* Furthermore, the jacket "was bereft of any external indicia of ownership — there was no lettering, nametag, or the like to alert the searchers." *Id.* The jacket "could have been designed for a man or a woman or without regard to gender." *Id.* The officers thus "did not know — nor did the circumstances prompt them to inquire — who owned the jackets found in the entry room." *Id.*

The prosecution will likely argue that the search of Sophie's backpack was lawful. First, the prosecution can argue Sophie had a relationship with the premises. Just as spending the night and answering the door in a robe in *Giwa* suggested more than a mere temporary presence, Sophie's actions of taking a shower and getting dressed at the apartment suggest more than a mere temporary presence at the apartment. Sophie felt so comfortable at the apartment that she chose to shower and dress there in lieu of her own home. At the time the officers arrived, she was stretched out on the couch, with wet hair, and her shoes off. Sophie was so comfortable with the apartment that she engaged in activities typically done only by occupants of a home. Thus, Sophie was not merely "passing by" or a "casual visitor" to the apartment. She had a relationship with the premises.

Second, the prosecution can argue Officer Braxton did not have notice that the backpack belonged to Sophie. Like the jacket in *Gray*, which was located in an "outer room," Sophie's backpack was located in an "outer room." It was at the front door. In fact, it was next to a pair of men's shoes, indicating it belonged to one of the two male occupants listed on the search warrant. Furthermore, just as the nylon jacket in *Gray* had no lettering or nametag to alert the officers about

Application:
Losing
Argument #1

Application:
Losing
Argument #2

the jacket's ownership, Sophie's backpack had no lettering or name tag to alert Officer Braxton that the backpack belonged to Sophie. Sophie's backpack had an "H" and said "Crimson;" however, neither of these markings suggest the backpack belonged to Sophie rather than one of the male occupants. The connection between an "H" and "Harvard" is too remote to expect Officer Braxton to know they were the same. The backpack was just like the red nylon jacket in *Gray*, which could have equally belonged to anyone at the apartment. Thus, the circumstances did not give Officer Braxton adequate notice that the backpack belonged to Sophie.

The prosecution's arguments are likely to fail. A court will likely find the search of Sophie's backpack was not lawful. First, Sophie did not have a relationship with the premises because Sophie was a mere passerby with only a temporary presence at the apartment. Unlike the visitor in *Gray*, who was found at the premises at 3:45 a.m. in the middle of a drug bust, Sophie was merely visiting friends in the afternoon before a football game. There was nothing unusual about her visit and Officer Braxton had no reason to believe she was involved in any criminal wrongdoing. Sophie was simply stopping by the apartment to take a quick shower and have a beer before heading to a football game. She planned to stay for a short time and nothing about her circumstances suggested she was more than a casual visitor who planned a temporary visit to see her friends. Sophie's decision to take a shower does not take away her right to be free from unlawful search and seizure. The defendant's decision in *Giwa* to spend the night at the premises alone, without the occupants present, made his relationship with the premises more like that of an occupant. Here, Sophie did not spend the night at the apartment and was not alone in the apartment. Merely sitting on a couch to have a beer at her friends' apartment prior to attending a football game does not equate her to an occupant. Further, showering does not equate one to the status of an occupant. It is common for a visitor, especially a college student, to take a quick

Application:
Winning
Argument #1

shower at a friend's place right before going out. Sophie was simply in a hurry and only planned to stay at the apartment temporarily before heading to the game. Thus, Sophie's circumstances suggest her stay was temporary and she did not have a relationship with the premises.

Second, Officer Braxton was put on notice that the backpack belonged to Sophie. Unlike the location of the red nylon jacket in *Gray*, which was in an "outer room," Sophie's backpack was not in an "outer room." It was at the front door. The location of Sophie's backpack at the front door indicated it could belong to a visitor at the premises. The officers knew only two occupants lived at the apartment, yet saw three individuals inside. Thus, Officer Braxton knew a visitor was present. Occupants do not typically leave their backpacks at the front door, but are more likely to bring belongings into a bedroom or to a kitchen table. Visitors, on the other hand, are more likely to drop a backpack at the door as they walk in. Thus, the location of the backpack indicated it could belong to Sophie. Furthermore, although the backpack was sitting next to a pair of men's shoes, the markings on the backpack indicated it belonged to Sophie and not one of the male occupants. Unlike the jacket in *Gray*, which had no nametag or lettering to indicate who owned the jacket, Sophie's backpack contained markings that suggested it was owned by Sophie. The backpack was marked with the Harvard insignia "H" on the front, followed by the word "Crimson." The color of the backpack also matched the colors of Harvard College: red, black, and grey. Sophie was wearing a Harvard t-shirt. The two male occupants, who were the subject of the warrant, did not have any Harvard insignia on their clothing. In fact, the two male occupants both had on Boston University insignia. Most residents of Cambridge, where the search took place, are familiar with the Harvard "H" and the Harvard colors. The apartment was also in close proximity to Harvard College, so officers who work in the area would know the "H" emblem stood for "Harvard." The backpack is thus unlike

Application:
Winning
Argument #2

the red nylon jacked in *Gray,* which could have belonged to anyone in the apartment. The location of the backpack and Harvard insignia on the backpack tied the backpack directly to Sophie. Therefore, Officer Braxton had sufficient notice that the backpack belonged to a visitor.

Therefore, a court will likely find the officer's search of Sophie's backpack was unlawful.

Conclusion

V. Conclusion

A court will likely find that Sophie's backpack was unlawfully searched. Sophie was a mere visitor to the apartment who was passing by on the way to a football game and had no relationship to the premises. Furthermore, Officer Braxton was put on notice that the backpack belonged to Sophie because it had Harvard insignia and Sophie was the only one in the apartment wearing a Harvard t-shirt. Thus, the search was likely unlawful.

INDEX